INWARD LIES THE ....

INWARD LIES THE WAY

GERMAN THOUGHT AND THE NATURE OF MIND

—

FOUR ESSAYS BY

STEPHEN CROSS AND JACK HERBERT

TEMENOS ACADEMY

TEMENOS ACADEMY PAPERS NO. 26

This paper comprises four lectures,
revised in book form,
delivered to the Temenos Academy
at the Essex Unitarian Church, London
during the Michaelmas Term 2002

First published 2008 by
The Temenos Academy
16 Lincoln's Inn Fields
London WC2A 3ED

www.temenosacademy.org

Registered Charity No. 1043015

ISBN 978–0–9551934–2–2

The Temenos Academy wishes to thank an anonymous donor
for generously sponsoring the publication of this book.

Cover image
Head, lithograph 1960,
by Cecil Collins
© Tate, London 2007

Typeset by
Agnesi Text, Hadleigh

Printed in the United Kingdom at
Smith Settle, Yeadon

We dream of travelling through the
universe: is then the universe not in us?
The depths of our spirit we do not know.
Inward lies the mysterious way.

Novalis: *Pollen*

(*Wir träumen von Reisen durch das Weltall:
ist denn das Weltall nicht in uns? Die Tiefen
unsers Geistes kennen wir nicht. – Nach
Innen geht der geheimnisvolle Weg.*)

CONTENTS

Preface

THE essays contained in this book arise out of lectures delivered at the Temenos Academy, London, during the autumn of 2002; two further lectures given by the late John Allitt in the same series, of much interest but thematically different and concerned with the Bavarian Illuminati and the music of Johann Simon Mayr, have not been included.

The four essays brought together here attempt to convey the different orientation of German thought from that to which we are generally accustomed in English-speaking countries. It is not widely appreciated that the approach of German thought to the world around us, and especially to the way in which our relationship with that world is understood, is significantly different from that of our own main tradition. Responding in part to the alchemical thought of the medieval and Renaissance periods, so richly developed in their lands, German-speaking peoples developed a way of understanding the world—and especially our relation to it—which is often closer to that found in India and other parts of Asia than it is to the empiricism of the British tradition or the rationalism of the French. It was the unexpected discovery of this similarity with Indian modes of thought which, as the eighteenth century drew to a close, gave rise in Germany to the idea of an Oriental Renaissance—that is to say, a rebirth of the spirit, brought about by contact with the thought of the Orient, which would equal in significance the revival which flowed from the rediscovery of classical antiquity during the Italian Renaissance. This largely forgotten yet significant episode in the history of ideas, which left upon German culture a permanent impression, forms the subject of our opening chapter.

For the German mind, as for the Indian, it is our processes of perception and conception which condition and to a significant degree create the world we live in. On this view, the mind—'what goes on in our head', as Schopenhauer bluntly put it—is primary, and the world which we all see and experience appears and exists only in and through our consciousness. For the predominant British tradition, on the other hand, things are the other way round and the world is understood in a different manner: the external world and the objects which constitute it are taken to be given and fixed realities, every bit as real as the subject who perceives them. It is of course true (and the poet and founder of the Temenos Academy, Kathleen Raine, spent her life in reminding us of this) that another tradition of British thought, centred on such figures as Berkeley, Blake, Coleridge, Shelley and more recently W. B. Yeats, viewed the world very differently and in a way which is much closer to that of the Germans. But it is not the *dominant* tradition in Britain, as its counterpart is in German-speaking areas. For the mode of thinking which, by and large, has dominated in Britain, the world of external facts is what is primary, while the human mind reacts and adapts to this as best it can. Subjective factors are seen as peripheral and of relatively little import in comparison with a world made up of solid, quantifiable, objective realities existing in time and space and quite independently of ourselves. In spite of the fact that this view has come under serious challenge as a result of developments in physics during the last century, this strongly rooted empiricism continues in practice to reign comparatively undisturbed. Objects exist 'out there'. They are 'things', existing quite apart from the subject—the stone, for example, which Dr Johnson kicked in the belief that in doing so he was providing an adequate refutation of Berkeley's idealism.

For the mind steeped in German ways of thought this is no more than the naive realism of 'common sense', as becomes clear in the chapter on Jung with which the present book closes. Rather than the outward-looking pattern of thought of which the physical sciences and their exploitation by technology are the sign, German thinkers have placed a strong emphasis upon the inner life of human beings and the power of the mind to creatively affect the external conditions we experience. From a German standpoint the world-view of British empiricism lacks unity, for it presents us with a fragmented universe of separate objects which stand in opposition to each other as well as to the subject, who thus becomes but one more object in the world— a quantifiable unit in a vast material structure, as Kathleen Raine has put it. This view thus tends towards a utilitarian devaluation of both subject and object, eroding our grasp of our own humanity; this is one of the major issues with which Heidegger's thought is concerned. If a broad generalization be permitted, one might say that while the world-view of the dominant British tradition is primarily mechanical, the German tradition tends towards a more organic and holistic view; the role played in cognition by the subject is more strongly emphasized, and the external world is seen as mentally shaped, linked to the consciousness of the subject and to a considerable degree its reflection. Without this understanding, German thought will often seem arbitrary and strange to us; with it, a fresh vision of the world and of our relation to it opens up.

Even in earlier times the great figures of German thought generally looked inwards, seeking to explore not so much the outer world but man's inner world and its relations to what was around him; we need think only of Meister Eckhart, Nikolaus Cusanus, Paracelsus and Jakob Boehme. And so when around the middle of the eighteenth century the energies which had thus been gathering strength in German-speaking areas of Europe came into contact with the outwardly directed thought of the Enlightenment, deriving from British as well as French sources, an unprecedented cultural explosion took place. This initially took the form of the *Sturm und Drang* ('Storm and Stress') movement in literature, then of various forms of philosophical idealism, and finally of the broader Romantic movement which so deeply affected the outlook of the nineteenth century. The new vision, which found its most characteristic expression in the spheres of philosophy, poetry and music, explored man's inner world while asserting his power to shape the outer world of experience. The subject was no longer felt to be at the mercy of the world around him;

he could rise above it, dominate it and even to a considerable extent re-create it, for the external world grows out of the consciousness of the subject and is its reflection.

This decisive and powerful re-affirmation of the inner world and of the centrality of the subject, standing in sharp contrast both to the rationalism of the Enlightenment and to the scientific–industrial revolution cultivated in Britain, ushered in a period of continuous creativity the like of which had not been seen since the Italian Renaissance. For two centuries and across a wide spectrum of human activity, not excluding the physical sciences, a host of key figures appear in German-speaking areas, ranging from Herder, Kant, Novalis, Goethe and Beethoven, through Schopenhauer, Caspar David Friedrich and Wagner, to such later representatives as Kafka, Rilke, Freud, Einstein, Schrödinger, Heisenberg, Heidegger and Jung. All of these, whatever their differences, may be seen as bound together by an awareness of the mind's primacy and its immense imaginative powers; Einstein, for example, stated that 'Knowledge is limited, but imagination encircles the world. Imagination is more important than knowledge', and we find Rilke, in his *Letters to a Young Poet*, writing: 'You are looking outwards and that, above all, is what you should not now be doing. Nobody can advise and help you—nobody! There is only one course to take: *go within yourself.*'

Within the confines of the present short work it is possible only to touch on a few aspects of this remarkable period; but we hope that our explorations into the early Romantic writers of the 'Oriental Renaissance', Goethe's *Faust* and its roots in the alchemical tradition, the challenging figure of Schopenhauer, and the psychological insights of Jung, will convey to the reader something at least of the complexity and transformative power of German thought, of the manner in which it differs from our own dominant tradition, and, last but not least, of the way in which it parallels that other stream of British thought which flows from Blake to Yeats and Kathleen Raine.

1

The German Romantics and the Vision of India

Stephen Cross

LET us begin with an episode of literary history, long forgotten by all but a few specialists. It was inspired by the idea that Europe stood on the threshold of a second Renaissance—an *Oriental Renaissance* this time, which would bring about a renewal of culture and intellectual life equal in scope and splendour to the great achievements of the Italian Renaissance. This idea swept through literary and philosophical circles in Europe, and above all in Germany and France, during the years between 1795 and 1810, and all of the principal figures with whom we are concerned in this chapter—Herder, Novalis, Schelling and Friedrich Schlegel—were significantly involved.

Here are a few passages from writers of the time which will convey some idea of the hopes then entertained. Novalis, in his *Spiritual Songs* (*Geistliche Lieder*), writes: 'The East is lighting up in the distance, the past is being restored, and India shall, even in the very North, flower with joy for the Beloved.'[1] Schelling in a letter of 1806 declares: 'We cannot do without [the Orient]. Open, free communication with it must exist, so that the old life of the fifteenth and sixteenth centuries may better return.'[2] Echoing the same idea, the French scholar and traveller Anquetil Duperron writes in a work published posthumously in 1808: 'We stand, in relation to Sanskrit, where Europe stood in relation to Greek at the time of the fall of Constantinople.'[3] In the

---

1. Cited in R. Schwab, *The Oriental Renaissance: Europe's Rediscovery of India and the East, 1680–1880* (Columbia University Press, New York, 1984), p. 207.
2. Letter to Windischmann of 18 December 1806, as translated in J. W. Sedlar, *India in the Mind of Germany: Schelling, Schopenhauer and their Times* (University Press of America, Washington DC, 1982), p. 42. German text in G. L. Plitt (ed.), *Aus Schellings Leben in Briefen* (Hirzel, Leipzig, 1870), vol. 2, p. 108.
3. As translated in Schwab, *Oriental Renaissance*, p. 13.

same year Friedrich Schlegel, in his important study *On the Language and Wisdom of the Indians*,[4] writes as follows: 'The Renaissance of antiquity promptly transformed and rejuvenated all the sciences; we might add that it rejuvenated and transformed the world. We could even say that the effects of Indic studies, if these enterprises were taken up and introduced into learned circles with the same energy today, would be no less great and far-reaching.'[5] And ten years later Schopenhauer, in the Preface to *The World as Will and Representation*, asserts that knowledge of the Upanishads is 'the greatest advantage which this still young century has to show over previous centuries, since I surmise that the influence of Sanskrit literature will penetrate no less deeply than did the revival of Greek literature in the fifteenth century.'[6]

This, then, was the idea which animated the brightest spirits of the day, an *Oriental Renaissance*, an intellectual and spiritual revolution in the life of Europe like that which had taken place in fifteenth-century Italy, but based not on the recovery of Greek and Latin texts but on the literature and philosophical knowledge of India. 'In the first ardor of their discoveries', wrote the French cultural historian Edgar Quinet some years later, 'the orientalists proclaimed that, in its entirety, an antiquity more profound, more philosophical, and more poetical than that of Greece and Rome was emerging from the depths of Asia.'[7] Quinet knew what he was talking about, for as a young man he had witnessed the ferment of ideas at Heidelberg University. What was it, then, which brought about this wave of excitement and enthusiasm among the young poets and thinkers of Germany, these sanguine hopes of a great cultural renewal?

4. *Über die Sprache und Weisheit der Indier*; for the German text of this work see E. Behler and U. Struc-Oppenberg, *Kritische Friedrich-Schlegel-Ausgabe*, vol. 8 (Thomas-Verlag, Zurich, 1975), pp. 105–433. For an English translation see E. J. Millington, *The Aesthetic and Miscellaneous Works of Frederick von Schlegel* (Henry Bohn, London, 1849), pp. 425–526.

5. As translated in Schwab, *Oriental Renaissance*, p. 13. Original text in Behler and Struc-Oppenberg, *Schlegel-Ausgabe*, vol. 8, p. 111.

6. *The World as Will and Representation*, trans. E. F .J. Payne (Dover Publications, New York, 1969), vol. 1, p. xv.

7. Cited in Schwab, *Oriental Renaissance*, p. 11.

The answer is to be found in an unexpected quarter: among the British administrators and traders in eastern India. For it was here, in the distant land of Bengal, that a handful of men associated with the great East India Company, had, around 1780, begun to unlock the treasure chest of Indian literature. The key to this was the ancient classical language of India, Sanskrit. Up until then it was quite unknown to Europeans, a mystery.[8] Yet in Sanskrit was preserved the sacred literature of India, her treasures of poetry and drama, and the legal code by which Hindu society was organized. It was especially to this latter that the British wanted access, for Warren Hastings, the Governor-General, had recognized that in order to govern effectively in Bengal the British had to incorporate Hindu law into the system by which they ruled, and this could not be done without a knowledge of Sanskrit.

To obtain this was no easy matter. Not only was Sanskrit a strange and difficult language to Europeans, but because it was the language of their sacred texts, the *Vedas*, the Brahmins of India were reluctant to teach it to others. At length British prestige and influence was able to overcome this obstacle and a young jurist, Charles Wilkins, was sent to the ancient city of Benares to learn the sacred language from the renowned *pundits* there. In this way the language barrier was broken through, and, by fortunate coincidence, very soon afterwards there arrived in Bengal a man of high talent able to take full advantage of the new opportunity. He was William Jones (later Sir William Jones), and he arrived in Calcutta at the end of 1783 to assume the role of Chief Justice in the recently established Supreme Court of Judicature. Jones, a friend of Gibbon, Edmund Burke and Dr Johnson, was a man of wide culture and a gifted linguist already known for his translations of Arabic and Persian poetry. He quickly seized the opportunity offered by Wilkins's newly acquired knowledge to add Sanskrit to his accomplishments. Others among the British in Bengal were also keen to explore the language, history and civilization of the ancient land they had come to, and within a few weeks of Jones's arrival they had

8. The only exceptions were a small number of Jesuit missionaries who during the seventeenth and eighteenth centuries took steps to learn Sanskrit. Schlegel mentions two of these in the Preface to *On the Language and Wisdom of the Indians*, but in general their efforts were stillborn and gathered dust in the Vatican library.

banded together to form the Asiatic Society of Bengal. From then on a steady stream of translations and essays flowed to Britain and the rest of Europe. Suddenly the literature and philosophical and religious thought of India started to come into focus for the West.

The first work to appear in translation was the *Bhagavad Gita*, translated by Wilkins and published in 1785. It came into the hands of William Blake among others—we know this because Blake left a drawing, now unfortunately destroyed, entitled *Mr. Wilkins translating the Bhagavat Geeta*. In 1789 Jones himself published *Shakuntala, or the Fatal Ring*, his translation of a drama by Kalidasa, one of the greatest of India's poets who is thought to have lived in the fifth century AD. A little later came Jones's translation of another literary masterpiece, Jayadeva's *Gita Govinda*, a long, glittering poem written in the eleventh century and highly prized in India, in which the love of Radha and Krishna is described in terms of a glowing erotic mysticism. Tragically, Jones died at the beginning of 1794 after barely ten years in India; but later in that same year his translation of the Hindu legal code, *The Laws of Manu*, setting out the entire organization of traditional Indian society, was published posthumously.

These works together with certain others produced a dramatic effect among the young poets and philosophers of the early Romantic period in Germany. The publications of the Asiatic Society were eagerly seized upon and retranslations into German quickly followed. Jones's *Shakuntala* was put into German by a disciple of Herder, Georg Forster, and the result was received with tremendous acclaim; Wilkins's *Bhagavad Gita* was also translated into German and received with great interest. A German version of *The Laws of Manu* was made, and the *Gita Govinda* was translated not once but twice.

No less important was the stream of essays which appeared in the journal of the Asiatic Society, *Asiatick Researches*. Published in Calcutta and reprinted in London, it ran through successive editions. French and German translations were made of its contents and most of the leading figures of German thought, from Herder and Goethe to Schopenhauer and Hegel, were familiar with it. In both Germany and France periodicals kept abreast of the new developments: the

Asiatisches Magazin and the Schlegel brothers's short-lived but influential publications *Europa* and *Athenaeum* in Germany, and in France the *Magasin Encyclopedique* and *Décade philosophique.*

In the pages of *Asiatick Researches* appeared Sir William Jones's celebrated assertion that the resemblance of the ancient Sanskrit language of India to Greek and Latin could not have been produced by accident and that all three ancient tongues must have sprung from a common source—while the old Germanic, Persian and Celtic languages very probably form part of the same family. With this epoch-making claim an entirely new concept was born: that of an Indo-European group of languages. It was a momentous idea, and the Germans in particular were fascinated. A common cultural inheritance of immense antiquity and perhaps even a common racial origin were implied and the idea of India as an *Urheimat*, a land of primal origin, began to take root. A dramatically new vision of the history of the world beckoned; for a Europe anchored to biblical chronology and the constricted view of history which went with it the implications were prodigious.

Simultaneously, the advanced level which literature had attained in ancient India became clear. Initially it was Jones's translation of the poetic drama *Shakuntala* which made this apparent. Its sudden appearance from so utterly unexpected a quarter as India took Europe by surprise; it seemed almost a miracle and quickly earned for Jones an international reputation. Kalidasa is perhaps the greatest dramatist India has produced—Jones speaks of him as 'our illustrious Poet, the Shakespeare of India'—and the refined taste exhibited by his drama, the literary skill with which it is executed, and the pathos of the situation it depicts amazed and moved its German readers and indeed all of cultured Europe. Goethe was captivated by it and as usual succeeded in catching the mood of the moment, writing in 1791 lines which soon became famous:

Willst du die Blüthe des frühen, die Früchte des späteren Jahres,
Willst du, was reizt und entzückte, willst du, was sättigt und nährt,
Willst du den Himmel, die Erde mit Einem Namen begreifen;
Nenn'ich, Sakontala, dich, und so ist Alles gesagt.

Wouldst thou the young year's blossoms and the fruits of its decline,
And all by which the soul is charmed, enraptured, feasted, fed,
Wouldst thou the earth and Heaven itself in one sole name combine?
I name thee, O Shakuntala! and all at once is said.[9]

So impressed was Goethe by the play that he planned to write an adaptation of it for the German stage. As things turned out this project was not realized, but the Prologue of *Faust*, which he drafted about 1797, is modelled on the witty dialogue between stage-manager and actors which forms the Prologue of *Shakuntala*. Schiller too borrowed from Kalidasa. The latter's poem *The Cloud Messenger*, a translation of which appeared in *Asiatick Researches*, provided the inspiration for the celebrated and moving passage in Schiller's play of 1801, *Maria Stuart*, in which the unhappy, exiled queen calls on the southward-flying clouds to bear her greetings to the distant land of France in which the happy years of her youth had been passed.[10]

But it was not only the skill of a great dramatist and the fascination of an unfamiliar and exotic world which drew Germans towards the literature of India at this time. It was also the ideas they found there. About a decade after the publication of *Shakuntala* a still more remarkable work appeared. This was the earliest translation into a European language of the Upanishads and it appeared in Latin in 1801 under the title, *The Oupnek'hat*—a Persianized form of the Sanskrit word, *Upanishad*.[11] This weighty, two-volume publication was by any stan-

9. H. Düntzer (ed.), *Goethes Werke* (5 vols.; Deutschen Verlags-Anstalt, Stuttgart and Leipzig, 1882), vol. 1, p. 109. The translation is that of H. G. Rawlinson in his essay 'India in European Literature and Thought', in G. T. Garratt (ed.), *The Legacy of India* (Oxford, 1937), p. 33.

10. Rawlinson, in Garratt, *Legacy of India*, pp. 32–3.

11. Strictly speaking, the *Oupnek'hat* was not quite the first European translation of the Upanishads. Anquetil Duperron published a French translation of four of these texts in 1786, but finding French unsatisfactory for this purpose he subsequently turned to Latin (see Schwab, *Oriental Renaissance*, p. 52). Wilhelm Halbfass points out that a translation of the brief *Isa Upanishad* was published in 1799 in an edition of the collected works of Sir William Jones; see W. Halbfass, *India and Europe: an*

dards an extraordinary work and more will be said of it in connection with Schopenhauer in a later chapter. It had nothing to do with the British based in Bengal but was the achievement of one man, the remarkable French orientalist Anquetil Duperron, already famous for his recovery and translation of the lost Zoroastrian scriptures. *The Oupnek'hat* created great interest on account of the surprising resemblance which the doctrines it contained showed to recent developments in German philosophical thought. In the notes accompanying his translation Anquetil Duperron drew attention to the similarities it shows to the new and radical ideas of Kant. He calls upon the thinkers of his day, naming Goethe, Wilhelm von Humboldt, Schiller, Fichte, Jacobi and Reinhold among others, to study the teachings of the *Upanishads*, and to see in them not just an interesting philological curiosity but a philosophical challenge of a vital and contemporary kind.[12] Anyone who carefully examines Kant's thought, he claims, will find that it is not far from the teachings of the Brahmins which 'lead man back to himself and comprise and focus him within himself'.[13] It was seen in Germany that the teaching of the Upanishads, and the idea of *Maya* or Illusion which they contain, are essentially in agreement with Kant's doctrine of the phenomenal nature of the world; Schelling and several of his followers (Rixner, Windischmann, Röth, Krause) studied *The Oupnek'hat* with much interest, and when Schopenhauer discovered it in 1813 it became of life-long importance to him.

Coming after the revelation of *Shakuntala*, the *Oupnek'hat* seemed to confirm the hopes placed in India. In the ancient texts which it translated the young Romantics of Germany were able to find much of their own sense of the transitory and illusory nature of earthly existence, and their own strong feeling that the true meaning of life lies outside the range of rational thought and in passing into some

---

Essay in Philosophical Understanding (State University of New York Press, Albany, 1988), p. 63.

12. Anquetil Duperron, *Oupnek'hat (id est, Secretum Tegendum)*, vol. 1 (Argentorati, Paris, 1801), p. 722.

13. As translated in Halbfass, *India and Europe*, p. 67.

greater whole beyond individual being.[14] The affinity of outlook implied by the relation of Sanskrit to the languages of Europe was seen to exist across a broad spectrum of cultural life, and Germans were able to discover in the old literature of India ideas and attitudes which were often close to their own. Here they found reflected not only their own *Weltschmerz*, or sense of the uncertainty and pain of worldly life, but also the same loving descriptions of nature and delight in connecting the joys and sorrows of human life with the natural world around us which feature so prominently in their own poetry and song.[15] Here too they could find a similar tendency towards abstract thought and the same high value placed upon careful scholarship. The extent of this affinity is sometimes surprising; it can be seen if we compare two of the brief aphoristic poems of the German mystic Angelus Silesias (Johannes Scheffler) with Indian texts. First, let us take one of the brief German poems:

O Men, become that which is the Essence, for when the world ends
Accident drops away, but Essence remains.[16]

And now a verse from an important Indian text, the *Yoga Vasishtha*:

14. An example is provided by Ludwig Tieck's vision in the Harz mountains in June 1792: 'It was not long until the sun rose. But where to find words that could even come close to an adequate description of what I saw, the miracle, the apparition facing me, changing my soul, my innermost being, transforming all my powers and drawing me irresistibly towards an invisible, divine, great nameless force. Unspeakable rapture suffused my whole being, I trembled, and rivers of tears, so tender and intense as I had never known, flowed from my eyes. I had to stand quite still to experience this vision completely, and as my heart trembled with exquisite joy, I was fully convinced, indeed I knew, that another blissfully loving heart touched my bosom'. As cited by Robert Minder in 'Metamorphoses of the Tieck-Image', in R. Grimm (ed.), *Romanticism Today: Friedrich Schlegel, Novalis, E. T. A. Hoffmann, Ludwig Tieck* (Inter Nationes, Bonn-Bad Godesberg, 1973), pp. 64–5.

15. M. Winternitz, *A History of Indian Literature*, trans. S. Ketkar (University of Calcutta, 1963), vol. 1, pp. 6–7.

16. Angelus Silesius, *Der cherubinische Wandersmann*, ed. E. Brock (Diogenes, Zurich, 1979), p. 56. The German text reads:
    Mensch, werde wesentlich! denn wann die Welt vergeht,
    So fällt der Zufall weg, das Wesen, das besteht.

This is all that remains for you to know. Whatever there is in this universe will cease to be at the end of this world-cycle, leaving only the essence.[17]

It will be seen that the thought here is virtually identical. In another instance Angelus Silesius writes:

God, whose delight it is to be with you, O Man,
Prefers to come into your house when you are not at home.[18]

And in a text of the Advaita Vedanta tradition, the *Ashtavakra Gita*, we find the same thought:

Where there is 'I' there is bondage, where there is no 'I' there is release.[19]

When, in 1657, Angelus Silesius published his poems under the title *Der cherubinische Wandersmann* it is certain he had no knowledge of Indian religious and philosophical thought; his remarkable poetry arises entirely from within the German and Christian traditions. In the light of this inward relationship it is not surprising that we find one of the most significant and influential figures of the early decades of the nineteenth century, Wilhelm von Humboldt, carefully studying Sanskrit and publishing during the 1820s a series of articles on the *Bhagavad Gita*; in these he writes that this Indian text 'is perhaps the deepest and loftiest thing the world has to show' and confesses his 'gratitude to Fate for having permitted me to live long enough to come to know this book'.[20] Wilhelm Halbfass, in his book *India and Europe*, has drawn attention to the fact that all three of the most significant European philosophers of the earlier part of the nineteenth century,

17. Swami Venkatesananda (trans.), *Vasishtha's Yoga* (State University of New York Press, Albany, 1993), p. 451.
18. As translated in L. Forster (ed.), *The Penguin Book of German Verse* (Penguin Books, Harmondsworth, 1957), p. 145. The German text reads:
    Gott, dessen Wollust ist, bei dir, o Mensch, zu sein,
    Kehrt, wenn du nicht daheim, am liebsten bei dir ein.
19. *Ashtavakra Gita* 8.4, trans. H. P. Shastri (Shanti Sadan, London, 1978), p. 19.
20. Cited in Winternitz, *History of Indian Literature*, vol. 1, p. 15, and in Schwab, *Oriental Renaissance*, p. 59. See also Halbfass, *India and Europe*, pp. 86, 91.

Hegel, Schelling and Schopenhauer, were Germans who engaged exten-
sively and seriously with Indian thought, and that nothing comparable to this has taken place since.[21] However, the attitudes of these
three philosophers differed. Hegel kept himself well informed about
the Indian developments, and responded to Humboldt's essay on the
Bhagavad Gita in a review article (running to almost a hundred pages)
in which he discusses the world-view of the *Bhagavad Gita* and the
importance of Yoga and meditation in the Indian tradition.[22] Nevertheless, Hegel's thinking remained firmly centred in Europe: India
was the beginning of man's ascent but Europe was its culmination;
India was the past, and he likened the attraction which it exerted upon
his contemporaries to 'the deceptive smile of a woman'. Schelling,
as we have seen, was much interested by what he found in the
Oupnek'hat (and even more so by the *Gita Govinda*, as we shall see
shortly), but, as with Novalis, his interest in the Orient was subordi-
nated to the idea of a reborn and essentially esoteric Christianity.
Schopenhauer, on the other hand, regarded Christianity as deeply
flawed and already in decline, in spite of the profound truths it contained; as a result he was a persistent student of Indian thought in
both its Hindu and Buddhist forms and never wavered in the importance he attributed to it.

For the early Romantics of Germany, the discovery of Indian
thought came like a shower of refreshing rain, after the arid decades
during which the thinkers of the Enlightenment had dominated
Europe. In Germany eighteenth-century rationalism and the classic-
ism which went with it had sat in uneasy proximity—seen at its most
creative in Goethe—with deeply rooted indigenous traditions going
back to the hermetic and mystical thought of such men as Boehme,
Paracelsus and Meister Eckhart. To these traditions the Romantics felt
themselves drawn. Novalis was deeply interested in alchemy; Schelling, Tieck and many others in Jacob Boehme. The hollow deism of
the eighteenth century had become an intolerable burden and the

21. Halbfass, *India and Europe*, p. 100.   22. Ibid., p. 86.

new generation rebelled. But there was another factor in addition to this, for the enthusiasm for India drew much of its energy from a sub-terranean stream of ideas which can be traced back to the early days of the Renaissance in Florence. At the heart of this was the belief that somewhere in the East—the Renaissance tended to favour Egypt—there still lay hidden a primordial wisdom, the truly sacred element in religion from which Plato, Pythagoras, Orpheus, Hermes Trismegistus, Zoroaster and other great figures of the distant past had derived the deepest portions of their knowledge. This wisdom, which was also the lost essence of Christianity, could be recovered, it was thought, and by revealing the true meaning of human life would bring in its train a great rebirth of the spirit. This idea, which in the fifteenth century had inspired the work of Ficino and had subsequently come to be known as the *philosophia perennis*, had never quite been extinguished in Europe. Driven underground during the eighteenth century, it burst into flame again in the minds of the Romantics. The thoughts of Schelling, Novalis, Wilhelm and Friedrich Schlegel, Schopenhauer and many others with regard to India at this time therefore represent the resurgence of a deeply rooted tradition. The interest in India was not a matter of literary taste and philological enquiry only, but part of a great search for spiritual renewal. The turn towards the Orient was a quest for the pristine knowledge of the human race, for the lost paradise, indeed for one's own original spiritual nature.

Even before the appearance of the English translations from San-skrit late in the eighteenth century the precursors of the Romantic movement had started to look towards the East. Kant's friend and fellow citizen at Königsberg, J. G. Hamann (the so-called 'Magus of the North'), wrote as early as 1762 words which were to prove pro-phetic: 'How then will we revive the dead language of nature? Through pilgrimages to Arabia Felix, through crusades to the Orient and the restoration of its magic.'[23] And when in 1775 Nathaniel Halhed

23. J. G. Hamann, *Sämtliche Werke*, ed. J. Nadler (Vienna, 1950), vol. 2, p. 211. Cited in Schwab, *Oriental Renaissance*, p. 210.

published his book on Hindu society, *A Code of Gentoo Laws*, an English reviewer welcomed it by observing: 'Mr. Halhed has rendered more real service to his country . . . than ever flowed from all the wealth of all the *nabobs* by whom the country of these poor people has been plundered . . . Wealth is not the only, nor the most valuable commodity, which Britain might import from India.'[24]

It was, however, Herder who did most to give an early direction to the German awareness of India. Anticipating Hegel in some respects, he believed that human history, though it had no predetermined end, was an organic growth drawing its direction from the very nature of humanity. Blending Romanticism with nascent German cultural nationalism, he held that every nation, every people along with their traditions, was to be understood as a living, cohesive whole. Each nation was a unique individuality, growing from the trunk of humanity like the branches of a single gigantic tree; each contributed its own unique and valuable qualities to the great 'living human force', as he called it. Of this force he wrote: 'Because *one* form of humanity and *one* region of the earth were unable to contain it, it spread out in a thousand forms, it journeyed—an eternal Proteus—through all the areas of the earth and down through all the centuries'.

The classical idea, reflected so strongly by the France of Louis XIV and still the rationale behind the dominance of French ideas in eighteenth-century Germany, of a single valid culture, surrounded by barbarian approximations which had gradually to be civilized and absorbed within the central stream, was rejected. For Herder, there was no 'chosen people' or *Favoritenvolk* of this sort. Each people had their own wisdom, reflected in their traditions and national culture, and the self-fulfilment of each contributed to the development of mankind as a whole. The great organic growth which was human history and culture had its roots in the Orient, even though, Herder thought, its adolescence was to be found in Hellenism and its maturity in Rome. The Orient was Europe's own childhood: 'All

---

24. The passage is from an anonymous review published in the *Critical Review*, vol. 44 (September 1777). Cited in William Dalrymple, *White Mughals* (Harper-Collins, London, 2002), p. 40.

the peoples of Europe,' he wrote, 'where are they from? From Asia'.[25]

Herder's initial views about India probably owed more to intuition than to reliable information, but with the appearance of the first translations of Sanskrit texts his ideas found support. *Shakuntala, The Laws of Manu*, Wilkins's *Bhagavad Gita*, and the successive issues of *Asiatick Researches* all came into Herder's hands and the effect was considerable. Among his later writings we find a translation into German verse of a part of Wilkins's *Bhagavad Gita*, translations of some of the *Proverbs* of the Indian poet and grammarian, Bhartrihari, and an imaginary conversation in which an Indian Brahmin complains of the arrogance of Christian missionaries seeking to convert Hindus. But what, in the long run, was of most importance was that Herder vigorously took up and developed the idea of the relation suggested by Sir William Jones between Sanskrit and European languages. This seemed to imply an Indian origin for the peoples of Europe (we should remember that this was long before the invention of the Aryan Invasion theory), and Herder built up the notion of an Indian fatherland for the human race.

It was a period when *origins* were of much importance, and the idea spread like wildfire among the Romantics. Many thought that Sanskrit must be the original language of mankind, and India was seen as the cradle in which the divine infancy of the human race was nurtured: 'And do you know the land where infant mankind lived its happy childhood years, where stood the pillars of fire in which the gods descended to their darlings and mingled in their spirited play?' wrote Görres, one of the more enthusiastic of the Indophiles; 'Towards the Orient, to the banks of the Ganges and the Indus, it is there that our hearts feel drawn by some hidden urge.'[26]

As the idea of India took on increasingly mythical proportions a wave of new and fervent hope swept through the rising generation in Germany. It was felt that brilliant possibilities promising a great cultural renewal, a rebirth of the spirit and of poetry, had suddenly appeared. The enthusiam was especially strong at three centres: the

25. Halbfass, *India and Europe*, p. 70.
26. As cited by Halbfass, *India and Europe*, p. 73.

universities at Heidelberg and Jena, and the town of Weimar where
Goethe was established. In these places the Romantic movement was
in full flower and a galaxy of brilliant young minds took fire from one
another—Novalis, Schelling, Wilhelm and Friedrich Schlegel, Ludwig
Tieck, Schleiermacher, the poets Clemens Brentano and von Arnim,
Jean-Paul Richter, E. T. A. Hoffman, to name but some.

Prominent among the enthusiasts was a figure relatively unknown
today, but of considerable significance in developing the Romantic
interest in India. This was Friedrich Majer (1771–1818), a disciple and
friend of Herder. He was active at two of the principal strongholds of
Romanticism: at Jena, he was in touch with Herder, Schelling and
Schleiermacher; and at Weimar, both Goethe, mature and widely celebrated, and the youthful and unknown Schopenhauer formed part of
his audience. Majer was in spirit a thorough-going Romantic, but at
the same time a genuine orientalist. He made German translations of
Wilkins's *Bhagavad Gita* and Jones's *Gita Govinda*, both of which when
published at Weimar in 1802 produced a great effect in Romantic
circles. Among his other writings is a wide-ranging cultural history in
which India features prominently, *Zur Kulturgeschichte der Völker*, for
which Herder wrote the Foreword. Majer believed that the original
and true sources of the Western tradition were to be found in Indian
thought, and that the religious and philosophical situation in Europe,
left in ruins by the thinkers of the Enlightenment, could be restored
only by a return to these Indian origins. The Sanskrit literature which
had recently been revealed, he believed, represented 'the earliest
dreams of our species' ('*die Morgenträume unseres Geschlechtes*'), and
he held that what he called 'original monotheism' could be discovered
in the ancient Indian texts. Thus he writes:

It will no longer remain to be doubted that the priests of Egypt and
the sages of Greece have drawn directly from the original well of
India; that only Brahmanism can provide those fragments of their
teaching which have come down to us with the clarity which they
in themselves do not possess.[27]

27. Cited in Halbfass, *India and Europe*, p. 73.

Majer's influence was felt among the small group at Jena which formed the heart of the Romantic movement. Among its leading spirits were Schelling, Novalis and the two Schlegel brothers, and during the 1790s their relations were very close: 'You have been the High Priest of Eleusis for me,' wrote Novalis to Friedrich Schlegel in 1791, soon after they had first met in Leipzig. 'Through you I have learned of Heaven and Hell.'[28] All were filled with exultation by the idea, owing much to Herder and Majer, of an original and perennial spiritual knowledge which had been lost, but could now be recovered with the help of the wisdom of India. For Novalis, India stood for everything which the Enlightenment and 'the cold, dead Spitsbergen of that sitting-room reason' which informed it were not.[29] The immense wastes of ice of that barren island of the north symbolized for the Romantic imagination the deadly grip of Reason, as it freezes into immobility the human spirit.[30]

It is not always easy, two centuries later, to comprehend the enthusiasms and euphoria of the early Romantics in Germany, but there is no doubt that these arose in part from the way in which they understood the Kantian philosophy. They had grasped from this that perception is not something which flows from an external cause to a merely passive recipient, but that the subject himself plays a vital role in the creation of perceptions and hence of the world of experience—Kant himself had spoken of the 'productive imagination'.[31] As Schopenhauer too would subsequently claim, the mind places its own interpretation upon the bare sensations which come to it, combining the information derived from the separate senses so as to form a unity, a perceived object. Hence it creates the world we know: the world each one of us experiences—whatever else there might be that lies behind

28. Cited in Schwab, *Oriental Renaissance*, pp. 207–8.

29. Cited in Halbfass, *India and Europe*, p. 74.

30. John Allitt, in a lecture at the Temenos Academy in 2002, has drawn attention to the use which Mary Shelley makes of this symbolism in her novel of 1818, *Frankenstein, or the Modern Prometheus*.

31. On the importance of the Subject for the early Romantic writers and their interpretation of the Kantian philosophy see R. Safranski, *Schopenhauer and the Wild Years of Philosophy*, trans. E. Osers (Harvard University Press, Cambridge, Mass., 1990), pp. 108–11.

it—is mentally conditioned and constructed. The empirical world was, for the Romantics, only mind solidified, only a mass of ideas seen as if they were external realities. In nature we see our own inner life, they thought, but crystallized and objectified.

So it was that the subject, the inner being of man himself, suddenly appeared in a new and amazing light. It was vitally creative: it is we, the Romantics believed, who create the world around us by the manner in which we perceive it, the way in which our creative imagination interprets and combines the sensations which come to us from without. Thus, in England, Blake could write: 'I know that This World Is a World of Imagination and Vision . . . Nature is Imagination itself . . . You certainly Mistake, when you say that the Visions of Fancy are not to be found In This World . . . This World is all One continued Vision of Fancy or Imagination.'[32]

Blake, it is true, was drawing from Berkeley rather than Kant, but his vision is very close to that of the Romantics in Germany. Up until that time the *subject* had, in European thought, tended to be lost in the external world: the outer world was what was real, it was the starting point, and the subject, the soul, was seen as trapped within it. Now the subject suddenly stepped forth in its full power and creative splendour, and the external world was found to be, so it was thought, little more than its effect: 'The exterior is the interior raised to a mysterious state', as Novalis put it.[33] We think—or, as Schopenhauer would have it, we will—the world into being; it is as we have imagined it into existence. And in consequence the Romantics believed that they could re-create the world in the image of their thought: 'Whatever I wish, I can do. Nothing is impossible for human beings,' declared Novalis.[34] They would do this by concentrating not upon external facts, but on the inner world of man. The key to a better world lay in changing the consciousness of the subject.

32. *The Complete Writings of William Blake*, ed. Geoffrey Keynes (London, 1969), p. 793. Cited by Kathleen Raine in *Berkeley, Blake and the New Age* (Golgonooza Press, Ipswich, 1977).

33. Cited in Safranski, *Schopenhauer*, p. 129.

34. Cited in Safranski, *Schopenhauer*, p. 130.

By means of the powerful action of poetry and the other arts the Romantics believed they would be able to transform the manner in which the world was perceived and therefore experienced. Poets and artists—'the unacknowledged legislators of mankind' in Shelley's phrase—would take up again their lost prophetic role and lead humanity to a world reborn in the imagination, a world of harmony and integration, of beauty, and of spiritual insight and meaning. 'I see already', wrote Schleiermacher in 1799 and perhaps with Novalis, Schelling and Schlegel in mind, 'a few significant figures initiated into these secrets returning from the holy place, who have only to purify and adorn themselves before they come forth in priestly garments.'[35]

In the eyes of the Romantics, Europe had sorely misused the sovereign power of the imagination during the Enlightenment and brought into being a world which was flat, prosaic, dehumanizing, dead. Humankind, in its early days, had known a world of a different kind, traces of which could yet be found in the fragments of myth, legend and anonymous poetry which had come down from the early races. First among these were the inhabitants of India. They too had created and lived in a world of a different kind from that which Europe now knew—a world in which men and women lived a life which was unified and whole, not split asunder into fragments; a world of poetry, myth and spiritual awareness. And now, quite suddenly and as if by a gift of grace, Europe had stumbled upon the ancient life of India. Here, so it seemed to men like Majer and Friedrich Schlegel, was a uniquely rich repository of the primordial wisdom of the past in which the magical 'childhood' of man could even now be rediscovered. Here was a source, a model, upon which contemporary Europe could draw, as by a mighty effort of the creative imagination her brightest spirits lifted men and women out of the materialistic depths into which they had sunk and placed them once again upon the glittering heights of poetry and esoteric wisdom.

Such were some of the ideas which around 1800 united the

35. As cited by Rudolf Otto in *Mysticism East and West*, trans. B. L. Bracey and R. C. Payne (New York, 1957), p. 219.

youthful Romantic thinkers of Germany. They built up a picture of India which, if largely mythical, nevertheless exerted great power on the imagination. To that distant and exotic land which had given birth to *Shakuntala* and the *Gita Govinda*, a land full of gods and their myths, were attributed all those qualities of profound spiritual knowledge and poetic insight which the Europe of their own day seemed so painfully to lack. The Orient took on a symbolic significance, India appearing as the realm of the lost unity of human existence and therefore the starting point for future regeneration. Here the search for the lost vision, the original revelation, could be commenced.

And yet Novalis, Schelling and Friedrich Schlegel all experienced a tension between their fascination with the image of India and what was at times a no less mythical image of an esoteric Christianity; a tension which it was their constant effort to resolve, and which was therefore continuously creative. In the case of Novalis, India never quite took on the same central significance that it had for Schlegel. It was the vision of a transformed Christianity which formed the heart of his inspiration. To Novalis, the modern fall from grace had begun with Luther's translation of the Bible, which had ushered in an age in which the letter tyrannized over the spirit, in which imagination and inner meaning were sacrificed to literalism and could no longer soar as they had in the Middle Ages.[36] For him, India and the Orient stood for what had then been lost: depth of feeling, true insight, the unfettered creative imagination and the inner resources of the spirit which could intuitively grasp those hidden realities which during the Enlightenment had ceased to exist for Europe. Novalis's own betrothed, the youthful Sophie von Kühn, seems to have symbolized for him these qualities; interestingly enough, within the circle of their friends she was known by the name *Shakuntala*.[37]

Novalis's novel *Heinrich von Ofterdingen*, fragmentary and unfinished

36. See Safranski, *Schopenhauer*, p. 64.
37. A. L. Willson, *A Mythical Image: The Ideal of India in German Romanticism* (Duke University Press, Durham, NC, 1964), p. 158.

though it is, is a pivotal work of the Romantic movement and we find references to the Orient scattered throughout its pages. In the fable of Atlantis, where the main themes of the novel are foreshadowed, we are introduced to an old king who rules a court full of poets and told that '*Er war aus einer uralten morgenländischen Königsfamilie entsprossen*' ('He sprang from a most ancient royal family of the East'); and later the hero, the young poet Heinrich, learns that '*Das Land der Poesie, das romantische Morgenland, hat Euch mit seiner süssen Wehmut begrüsst*' ('The land of poetry, the romantic Orient, has greeted you with its sweet melancholy').[38] Novalis believed that all things are interrelated and exist through one another—a very Indian viewpoint, as well as being deeply German. Could we but see aright we would find that all are dependent on one another and are held together in a network of subtle and indefinable bonds. Nature, which is really the reflection of the inner life of man, can be understood only as something which lives; a sensitive existence possessed as we are of emotional attributes: 'We search for the design of the world; yet we ourselves are that design', he wrote.[39] Only a poet, he thought, can understand Nature, for her true laws are the laws of the heart. Europe had lost its vision of the degree to which the spiritual and the material world are interwoven with each other, but in the writings newly available from India that vision is again found. Thus the Orient became an important element in his effort to fashion a new mythology—a mythology which would, he intended, combine the myths of many peoples and races into a rich and universal expression of the profoundest metaphysical truths.

For Novalis, much affected by the ideas of Herder,[40] India came to stand for that 'childhood' when humankind lived in a world of

38. Novalis, *Die Dichtungen*, ed. E. Wasmuth (Lambert Schneider, Heidelberg, 1953), pp. 43, 132.

39. Cited in Safranski, *Schopenhauer*, p. 129. See also Haywood, *Novalis*, p. 151.

40. Schwab (*Oriental Renaissance*, pp. 204–6) tells us that Novalis was 'enraptured' by Herder's *Ideen* as early as 1790, and the *Zerstreute Blätter* was among his frequent reading.

unbroken wholeness: '*Wo Kinder sind, da ist ein goldnes Zeitalter,*' he wrote—'Where there are children, there is a Golden Age.'[41] Poetry was born in the East. In the Golden Age of innocence and harmony which was India, poetry was not yet divided from religion: 'Poet and priest', he wrote, 'were in the beginning one, and only in later times did they become separated. Yet the true poet is always priest, just as the true priest ever remains a poet.' And he adds: 'And shall the future not bring about again the ancient state of things?'[42] What Novalis wishes to convey here is that a new Golden Age—perhaps more perfect than the first, because more consciously experienced—can be brought into being if only the unity and harmony of the world, veiled by the divisive processes of modern thought, can again be inwardly experienced. In this the poet-priests of the Romantic Revival would lead the way. The true poet is he who has the faculty of divining the hidden relationship between things and of expressing this relationship in perfect imagery: 'for only poets', the hero is told in *Heinrich von Ofterdingen,* 'can thoroughly understand that art of linking events together'.

In this way, through poetry's power to unite apparently disparate realms, the primordial unity and joy of life may be recovered and a new springtime of the spirit brought into being: '*dem Ende der Trübsale, der Verjungüng der Natur und der Wiederkehr eines ewigen goldenen Zeitalters*', Novalis wrote—'the end of misery, the rejuvenation of nature and the return of an eternal Golden Age'. The spirits of poetry and of religion, now reunited, would come together with the world of nature and of daily life—just as, in the fable of Atlantis in his novel, the princess who dwells within the castle of poetry unites in love with the simple youth who, in the forest beyond, lives close to nature. This mystic synthesis would be the renewal of the spiritual life of Europe, and its symbol was the wondrous Blue Flower which the young poet Heinrich dreams of at the beginning of the story.

41. Cited in Willson, *A Mythical Image*, p. 149.
42. 'Dichter und Priester waren im Anfang *eins*, und nur spätere Zeiten haben sie getrennt. Der echte Dichter ist aber immer Priester, so wie der echte Priester immer Dichter geblieben. Und sollte nicht die Zukunft den alten Zustand der Dinge wieder herbeiführen?' Cited in Willson, *A Mythical Image*, p. 148.

In the dreamed-of flower, the serene blue which Christianity traditionally associates with the Virgin Mary merges with the magic flower
found in the old legends of Thuringia, and these together join with
the blue lotus of India (the flower of the creator-god, Brahma, which
Novalis knew of from Forster's translation of *Shakuntala*) to form
exactly the kind of synthesis of diverse motives which Novalis so
much believed in. Thus the flower is an image of secret, hidden,
inward relationships; and just as in India the lotus opens its petals
before the morning sun, the Blue Flower unfolds its inner meaning as
the novel progresses. Ludwig Tieck, who handled Novalis's literary
papers after his death, stated that in the uncompleted part of the
novel Novalis intended that Heinrich would travel to the Orient, a
realm for which he had 'longed since childhood'; there fresh inventions would intermingle with materials drawn from Indian myths,
while the mystic glow of the Blue Flower would suffuse the whole
with its magic.[43] Even without this ending, the image of the flower,
and the atmosphere it generates with its gentle colour pervade the
entire tale, so that the Blue Flower became for many a symbol of the
Romantic ideal itself.

When we turn to Schelling we find that his early writings reflect
themes similar to those of Novalis. His essays on mythology, influenced by the ideas of Creuzer and Görres as well as Herder and Majer,
revolve around the concepts of an original but long-vanished monotheism, and of mythology as the history of human consciousness. For
Schelling too, India was a significant element in the attempt to discover the lost inner principle in religion and to bring to completion
the aspirations of Christianity. He held, in the words of Henri Lichtenberger, 'the conviction that a principle common to all religions existed
and that it was this principle which was the truly sacred element in
religion'.[44] The traces of primordial religion might be discovered, he
thought, in what was still known of pagan beliefs, and, perhaps in a
purer form, in the mythology of India. These, then, were not so
much a world to look back upon, as a door which opened into the

---

43. Willson, *A Mythical Image*, p. 165.
44. Lichtenberger, as quoted in Schwab, *Oriental Renaissance*, p. 219.

future.[45] It was necessary to recover the lost mysteries of the past; the myths of the Indians and of other ancient peoples, and the anonymous poetry which was the vehicle of these, beckoned like a treasure-house full of the jewels of ancient and universal wisdom. To cite Lichtenberger again:

> Schelling teaches that philosophy, born of poetry in the early days of the human race, must, after reaching full maturity, immerse itself once more, via the intermediary of the new mythology, in the ocean of poetry, and that Christianity, in its most recent inspiration, is a product of the Oriental spirit that brought forth the religion of India and in this way penetrated the entire Orient. Hence for the *choryphées* of Romanticism the Orient is gradually becoming . . . the homeland of that magical idealism that they dreamed of establishing.[46]

Schelling explored this theme in 1793 in his first published work, *On the Myths, Historical Legends, and Philosophemes of the World in Earliest Times.*[47] In it, and thinking probably in terms of the Romantic image of India (although India is not specified), he speaks of a people as yet untroubled by the demands of philosophy and living in close and innocent harmony with nature, as though with a benevolent mother. In the *System of Transcendental Idealism* of 1800 he places ancient India in the earliest of the three periods into which he divides history; this era, he claims, contained the noblest of humankind ever to blossom, and its greatness can only be surmised from the ruins it has left behind.[48] In the *Lectures on the Method of Academic Studies* of 1802 there is a general openness to India, and here Schelling praises the 'sacred texts of the Indians' and even goes so far as to suggest that

---

45. See E. Bréhier, *The History of Philosophy*, trans. W. Baskin (University of Chicago, 1968), vol. 6, p. 151. Also Schwab, *Oriental Renaissance*, p. 206.

46. As cited in Schwab, *Oriental Renaissance*, p. 492, n. 21.

47. *Über Mythen, historische Sagen und Philosopheme der ältesten Welt*. See Halbfass, *India and Europe*, p. 78; Willson, *A Mythical Image*, p. 114.

48. Willson, *A Mythical Image*, pp. 114 –15.

they are superior to the Bible.[49] He argues that the religion of India does not stand opposed to Christianity, but that on the contrary there exists a deep affinity between the two. He notes that, to the surprise of the missionaries, the Hindus were not amazed at the doctrine of the incarnation of God in Christ, but only surprised that such an event had not occurred more frequently in the West.[50] A few years later, in 1808, writing to A. W. Schlegel, he offers moral support for the creation of an institute for Indian and Oriental studies, saying: 'An entire Oriental Academy would not be too much. If it were in my power, some government would send a formal mission to the East . . . whose chief would be our esteemed *Brahmin*, Friedrich [Schlegel].'[51]

Yet in spite of such affirmations of interest and an acquaintance with most of the principal writings on India then available, it has been pointed out that specific references to Indian teachings are not frequent in Schelling's earlier works.[52] It is clear that he did not share the uncritical enthusiasm of many of his contemporaries; rather than this, he tried to fit India into a comprehensive picture of the development of world mythology which was conceived from a fundamentally Christian point of view.[53]

Among the Indian texts becoming available to Europe that which meant most to Schelling during his early period was the *Gita Govinda*, the poem of Jayadeva which William Jones had translated and which Majer had put into German in 1802. In a letter to A. W. Schlegel written in the following year Schelling speaks of the significance which this work has for him.[54] Jayadeva's long poem in twelve cantos

49. *Vorlesungen über die Methode des akademischen Studiums.* See H. von Glasenapp, *Das Indienbild deutscher Denker* (Koehler, Stuttgart, 1960), p. 34. Also Halbfass, *India and Europe*, pp. 100–101.

50. See Willson, *A Mythical Image*, pp. 113–16.

51. Letter of 26 August 1808, as translated in Sedlar, *India in the Mind of Germany*, pp. 42–3. See also Halbfass, *India and Europe*, pp. 100, and 485, n. 3.

52. Halbfass, *India and Europe*, p. 101.

53. See Halbfass, *India and Europe*, p. 104; Sedlar, *India in the Mind of Germany*, p. 125.

54. Sedlar, *India in the Mind of Germany*, p. 42; Schwab, *Oriental Renaissance*, p. 206 (see also p. 204, where Schwab claims that the poem marked a turning point in Schelling's thinking).

describing the different phases of the love-play between Krishna and Radha was also highly regarded by Goethe. For Schelling it took on a particular significance, for in it he believed that he saw expressed in the language of myth the central riddle of the cosmos: the mysterious polarity and mutual attraction which exists between the Absolute and the world of manifested and living forms. This was a mystery, he believed, which had first passed from India to Eygpt, thence into the Eleusinian mysteries, and finally to an inner and secret Christianity which had been known to Saint John and Saint Paul, after which time it had become lost.[55]

Schelling's position has been well summarized by the French historian of philosophy, Emile Bréhier, in these words: 'The content of revelation was not different from that of mythology nor from that of the religion to come. The natural gods were not made of a different substance from the supernatural God . . . Christ already existed before the revelation, but he was a cosmic force "in the world".'[56] This belief was no passing phase in the somewhat mutable thought of Schelling, for more than twenty years later in the fourth of the lectures forming the *Introduction to the Philosophy of Mythology* he again discusses these ideas. Here he writes:

Through the correspondences which exist between the Egyptian, Indian, and Greek mythologies, a common corpus of ideas in the explanation of mythology was finally revealed, in which the various theologies were at one . . . If one wished to obtain a conception of that original system, then the Mosaic scriptures would not be adequate for that purpose, and one would in fact have to search out the missings links in foreign theologies, in the fragments of Eastern religions and in the various mythologies.[57]

55. Schwab, *Oriental Renaissance*, p. 206.
56. Cited in Schwab, *Oriental Renaissance*, p. 218.
57. As translated by R. W. Stripling in his edition of Schelling's *Introduction to the Philosophy of Mythology* (privately printed, London, 1992), pp. 85–6.

Schelling was concerned to relate the mythologies of the world in a single and comprehensive scheme which would amount to a world history of religious thought.[58] His purpose was to elucidate the relationship between revealed religion (principally Christianity) and the mythologies of the ancient and Oriental worlds, and it is in this light that we can understand his interest in the Krishna of Jayadeva's poem. In his later writing the emphasis on revealed religion becomes stronger. India has its place in the scheme; it represents for Schelling a certain stage in the religious history of mankind, but it is neither the origin nor the culmination. In the end he decides that, together with China, India represents a stage of religious development subsequent to that of Egypt and immediately before that of Greece. We find then that, important as it was for him, especially in the early part of his career, Schelling was not overwhelmed by the Romantic image of India. He does not look for a rebirth of culture from contact with the Orient in the manner of many of his contemporaries. For Schelling it was not so much India as the entire body of mythology—hardly separated, in his view, from the expressions of poetry and art—which provided the key which would unlock the energies of the human spirit and bring about a rebirth of Europe.

Consequently, it was not Schelling but Friedrich Schlegel who became the pivotal figure in the German love affair with India. As a student of nineteen at Leipzig he had been fired with enthusiasm by *Shakuntala* and had wished to translate it. Now he shared with Schelling and Novalis the idea of a recovery of universal and perennial religion, and with Majer and Herder the notion of India as a land of origin. Like others of his generation, Schlegel saw the pleasure-seeking eighteenth century—'soul extinct but stomach well alive', in Carlyle's phrase[59]—as a time of crass materialism unworthy of the human spirit. He sought a way out of the spiritual torpor which had settled upon Europe, and seized with eager passion upon the literature of

58. Halbfass, *India and Europe*, p. 103.
59. Cited in R. N. Stromberg, *European Intellectual History since 1789* (Appleton-Century-Crofts, New York, 1968), p. 33.

India as a means to this end. 'It is in the Orient that we must seek the highest Romanticism', he roundly declared in 1800.[60] India, he believed, held the key to an understanding of the early history of humankind. In the profound idealism which was still preserved in the Vedic literature—and, at certain moments of history, had passed at least in part to the West—lay the ultimate source of the energies which had animated European civilization since ancient times:

> Without the constant recurrence of this animating principle European genius would never have soared so high, nor would its decline have been so sudden. Even the loftiest philosophy of the Europeans, the idealism of reason, as it is set forth by Greek philosophers, appears, in comparison with the abundant light and vigour of Oriental idealism, like a feeble Promethean spark in the full flood and heavenly glory of the noon-day sun, faltering and feeble, and ever ready to be extinguished.[61]

Schlegel, like others among the Romantics, was no mean scholar and he well understood that the meaning of the ancient texts could not be accurately grasped without a knowledge of the Oriental languages in which they were written. In 1802 (the year following the death of Novalis) he journeyed to Paris, both to lecture there on German literature and philosophy and in order to study Persian with the renowned French orientalist, A. L. de Chézy. Soon after his arrival an extraordinary stroke of good fortune enabled him also to study Sanskrit, and in fact to become the first German ever to master that language. In 1803 the Napoleonic wars suddenly flared up again and Alexander Hamilton, a founding member of the Asiatic Society and one of the small circle in Bengal who had obtained a thorough knowledge of Sanskrit, was detained in Paris while returning from India. Generously treated by the French authorities, he used his enforced leisure to

---

60. '*Im Orient müssen wir das höchste Romantische suchen*'; cited in Willson, *A Mythical Image*, p. 85.

61. As translated by Millington, *Works of F. von Schlegel*, p. 520.

teach Sanskrit to a group of interested persons. Schlegel was able to join this circle, writing from Paris to his brother: 'Everything is going wonderfully . . . I have learned a great deal . . . It happened that at just the right moment an Englishman, Hamilton, the only one in Europe apart from Wilkins who knows Sanskrit, and knows it thoroughly, assisted me.'[62]

In the former Bibliothèque Royale in Paris there were Sanskrit manuscripts, deposited by earlier travellers but never deciphered. Now Hamilton catalogued these while Schlegel worked intensely on translations. As he did so his ideas about India seemed to find confirmation, and he wrote enthusiastically in a letter to Ludwig Tieck: 'Here is the actual source of all languages, all the thoughts and poems of the human spirit; everything, everything without exception comes from India'.[63] Schlegel remained for several years in Paris and out of this time came his book, published in 1808, *On the Language and Wisdom of the Indians*; it was the first work in German in which the language, literature, and history of India are presented on the basis of original sources.[64] But as well as being a work of scholarship it was a statement of belief. The Romantic themes dominated, and Schlegel describes the way in which Europe found itself spiritually bankrupted by the thinkers of the Enlightenment:

Errors accumulated so rapidly that philosophy soon degenerated into mere scepticism; and, the vigour of human understanding becoming at length enfeebled by continued doubt and unbelief, philosophy next declined into empiric theory; the idea of a Supreme Divinity, if admitted in words, was denied in principle, till it became almost annihilated; and man, under the specious plea of confining himself within the sphere of utility and rationalism, cast

62. Letter of 15 May 1803, as translated in Schwab, *Oriental Renaissance*, p. 69. See also Schwab pp. 67–73, and Schlegel's own brief account in the Preface to *On the Language and Wisdom of the Indians* (Millington, *Works of F. von Schlegel*, p. 425).
63. Letter of 15 September 1803, as cited in Halbfass, *India and Europe*, p. 75.
64. E. Behler, cited in Halbfass, *India and Europe*, p. 75.

aside, as an erring and romantic impulse, that lofty spirit, intellect and sentiment, which alone distinguished him from the brute creation.[65]

After a catastrophe of this sort, Schlegel believed, renewal could come about only by searching deeply in the past. Specifically, it could be found in a recovery of that ancient wisdom of which India was the guardian, and which was at once the past and the future of humanity. In words still not without relevance, he writes:

In fact, nothing that exists can actually be called *new*; all must be kindled and inspired by ancient memories, instructed by departed genius, and formed and developed by antique power and energy. While, on the other hand, all those subtle reasoners, who live only in the present, and own no influence save that of the spirit of the day, have almost without exception, embraced the ruinous and destructive opinion that all should be created anew, and produced, as it were, from nothing. All knowledge of ancient philosophy is, therefore, fallen into contempt, and the taste for it is almost annihilated.[66]

With this state of affairs Schlegel contrasted the possibilities he had found in the course of his study of Indian thought, writing at the close of his book:

The too partial, almost wilful devotion to classical learning, which prevailed during the last century, drew men's minds too widely astray—too far from the sole source of lofty truth; but the study of Oriental literature, to us so completely novel in structure and ideas, will, as we penetrate more deeply into it, bring back a new idea of the Divinity, and restore that vigour to the intellect, that truth and intensity of feeling to the soul, which invests all art, science, and literature with new and glorious life.[67]

65. Millington, *Works of F. von Schlegel*, pp. 519–20.
66. Ibid., pp. 522.   67. Ibid., p. 526.

Here then, once again, is the theme of the Oriental Renaissance with which we began this chapter. If we now look back from the vantage point of the present we can see that the Oriental Renaissance did not fulfil the hopes placed in it in the immediate and dramatic manner envisaged. But we need not for that reason adjudge it a failure for, as later scholarship was to confirm, the bond between India and the peoples of Europe was deep and real. The intuitions of the early Romantic writers of Germany—of Herder and Majer, of Novalis, Schelling and the Schlegel brothers—were not a mere caprice, and the wave of enthusiasm for India and her past generated at this time had many later repercussions. With it a new element entered into the thought of German-speaking peoples, becoming a permanent part of their intellectual character. For since the time of the Oriental Renaissance the energies of many of Germany's finest minds have been directed towards India: not only Schopenhauer, to whom we will turn in a later chapter, but also the long line of great scholars who have led the West in the study of Indian thought and philology. Wilhelm Schlegel, the last survivor of the original group of Romantic enthusiasts, was the earliest of these, becoming Germany's first professor of Indology at Bonn in 1818; later in the nineteenth century we have such distinguished names as Christopher Lassen, Franz Bopp, Max Müller, Hermann Oldenberg, Paul Deussen. Poets and other creative artists were also deeply affected: we might take the example of Friedrich Rückert, not only a marvellous poet—he is perhaps best known in Britain as the writer of Mahler's *Kindertotenlieder*—but also a most accomplished Sanskrit scholar whose translations of Indian works into German have assumed the status of classics. Heinrich Heine also studied Sanskrit as a young man (under Wilhelm Schlegel), and several of his finest lyrics breathe the spirit of India.[68] Nor should we forget Wagner who, following the example of Schopenhauer, studied both the *Oupnek'hat* and the literature on Buddhism. For years his imagination was haunted by the idea of an opera centred on the life of the Buddha, and although this project was never realized it was the

---

68. Rawlinson mentions in this connection 'Die Lotusblume' and 'Auf Flügeln des Gesanges'; see Garratt, *Legacy of India*, p. 32.

source of much of the musical inspiration which eventually flowed into *Tristan and Isolde* and *Parsifal*.[69] In the twentieth century we see the same influence at work in writers and thinkers such as Hermann Hesse, Heidegger and Jung, each of whom shows in his own way the continuing effect of the thought of India and the Orient. Thus the intellectual adventure which originated with the early Romantic poets and thinkers of Germany continues to bear fruit.

This, then, is a brief outline of the effect which the discovery of the literature and thought of India had upon some of the brightest spirits of Germany some two hundred years ago, together with some of its lasting results. Let us now leave India for the time being; in discussing Schopenhauer in the third lecture we shall come back to it, but first we must turn to the greatest of German literary figures, Goethe, and to another important strand in the complex thought of the German-speaking world, the alchemical tradition.

69. For Schopenhauer's influence upon Wagner see Bryan Magee, *The Philosophy of Schopenhauer* (Clarendon Press, Oxford, 1997), pp. 350–402. Magee writes (p. 359) that the discovery of Schopenhauer's thought 'was the most important intellectual event in Wagner's life'. On the considerable effect which Indian, and particularly Buddhist, literature had upon Wagner see Schwab, *Oriental Renaissance*, pp. 438–44; Halbfass, *India and Europe*, p. 124; Magee, *Philosophy of Schopenhauer*, pp. 388, 396–7.

2

Goethe's *Faust* as *Opus Alchymicum*

Jack Herbert

THE title of this chapter, as well as in large measure its approach, derives from two statements made by C. G. Jung in his *Psychology and Alchemy*. The first runs: '*Faust* . . . consciously or unconsciously, is an *opus alchymicum*';[1] the second: '. . . alchemy had reached its final summit, and with it the historical turning point, in Goethe's *Faust*, which is steeped in alchemical forms of thought from beginning to end'.[2] Jung's first statement defines the nature of Goethe's drama in terms of two levels, conscious and unconscious; his second relates to the position of *Faust* within the alchemical tradition, while restating its essential nature. This latter quotation indicates that Goethe's play appears at the very end of that tradition, a last significant manifestation of it, and at the same time suggests that it represents a tipping over into something else. What Jung, I believe, is implying here is the transformation of alchemy into psychology—namely the psychologizing of alchemy or the alchemicizing of psychology.

Such a field fascinated Jung for most of his life—something only to be expected from a psychologist who first discovered, in what he termed 'philosophical alchemy', the true forerunner of psychology— 'philosophical', in order to distinguish it from that of the amateur 'chymist'[3] interested in metallic changes and results, but not the symbolic equivalents embodied in these and involving imaginative

1. C. G. Jung, *Collected Works* 12 (*Psychology and Alchemy*) (Routledge, 1957–79), p. 36, para. 42.
2. Ibid., p. 457, para. 558.
3. Cf. 'There is no doubt that the goal of the philosophical alchemist was higher self-development, or the production of what Paracelsus calls the *homo maior*, or what I would call individuation.' Ibid., 13 (*Alchemical Studies*), p. 179, para. 220.

projection. To give Jung's term a more explanatory context, and indirectly to bring in Goethe, let me quote from Johannes Fabricius's *Alchemy (The Medieval Alchemists and their Royal Art)*:

> The abundance of hallucinations, visions and dreams in Hermetic science helps to explain the paramount importance ascribed by the alchemists to man's powers of *imagination*. In the final analysis, the imaginative function appears to be the most important 'instrument' of the goldmakers, whose chemical operations seem to have served as projection-hooks for mental processes of unconscious origin. 'Imagination is the star in man, the celestial or supercelestial body,' says Ruland's *Lexicon Alchemiae* (1612) in its definition of *imaginatio*.[4]

Here we find explicit acknowledgement of alchemy's crucial role in boosting the status of the imagination in the West; and Martin Ruland, it should be noted, was a German alchemist whose dictionary was published in Frankfurt, Goethe's home town; so it is more than likely that the poet knew it. In any case, the earlier, more famous scholar and doctor, Paracelsus, is often referred to by Goethe, and Ruland's statement on the imagination as the star in man is basically Paracelsian. We should likewise point out that *Faust* is a supremely imaginative work, with Part II in particular possessing the nature of a phantasmagoria in its kaleidoscopic and cinematic shifts of scene. Taking into account the entire play with its two introductory episodes, *Vorspiel auf dem Theater (Prelude on the Stage)* and *Prolog in Himmel (Prologue in Heaven)*, the spectator undergoes a journey both complex and devious along different and varying imaginative levels; and referring back to our first quotation from Jung, this is 'consciously' as well as 'unconsciously' conceived. But to return for one moment to Johannes Fabricius's argument about imagination and its relation to philosophical alchemy:

4. Johannes Fabricius, *Alchemy (The Medieval Alchemists and their Royal Art)* (The Aquarian Press, 1989), p. 11.

In alchemy the adept comes to terms with 'true imagination' (Paracelsus's *imaginatio vera*) by means of the act of *meditation*. Ruland says of this: 'Meditation: The name of an internal talk of one person with another who is invisible, as in the invocation of the deity, or communion with one's self, or with one's good angel.'

The meditative aspect of the opus reveals the alchemists' understanding of their 'work' as a psychic process of transformation also, unfolding *pari passu* with the chemical process of transformation. In such a manner the alchemical laboratories took on the function of psychological laboratories as well. The effect was the symbolized chemistry of alchemy which, in the last analysis, represents an alchemy of the *mind*.[5]

Ruland's definition of what he understands by meditation is a most uncanny description of the world Faust himself actually inhabits—a world in which he is portrayed as constantly communicating with the beings and agents Ruland instances. For example, we find him continually invoking one spirit or another, as with the *Erdgeist* (Earth-Spirit) in the play's opening scene, or addressing invisible presences, as again with the *Erdgeist* at the beginning of the famous *Wald und Höhle* (*Forest and Cavern*) scene: '*Erhabner Geist, du gabst mir, gabst mir alles/Warum ich bat*' ('All things are come to me, O mighty spirit!/All that I asked you gave me').[6] And he can be seen and heard communing with himself throughout his various monologues. For essentially, as Faust is quite aware, his world is that of '*Das Doppelreich, das grosse*' ('the great double-realm'), the designation he uses at the close of Part II, Act I[7] to characterize both the reality of the

---

5. Ibid., p. 11.

6. The English translations from *Faust*, Part I, are by Philip Payne (Penguin Classics, 1976), unless otherwise stated; here p. 145. The German text, Parts I and II, is the *Hamburger Ausgabe* (hereafter HA) 3 (Verlag C. H. Beck, Munich, 1978); here lines 3217–18, p. 103.

7. The translations from *Faust*, Part 2, are by Walter Arndt (Norton Critical Edition, New York, 1976), unless otherwise stated. This also contains extensive notes, with a selection of interpretative essays, and has exactly the same line numberings as the HA; here line 6555, p. 201.

Emperor's Court and that of the magically evoked figures of Paris and Helen, summoned up for the Court's entertainment after his frightening descent to the domain of the mysterious Mothers.[8] Thus the double-realm encompasses not only the shades of the dead as well as spirits in general, but also the world of magical illusion, such as the Weimar Court theatre in Goethe's own time with its *laterna magica*,[9] and indeed that entire universe conjured up by the poet-magician. It is because of all this, I take it, that Rilke had avidly absorbed, then re-used this concept in the ninth of his *Sonnets to Orpheus*, Part 1, where the figure of the mythical Greek poet and images of earthly life mingle with shades from Hades: '*Erst in dem Doppelbereich/werden die Stimmen/ewig und mild*' ('Only in the double-realm/will these voices become/eternal and mild').[10] And we should also not forget that in the field of alchemy substances can be either 'fixed' or 'volatile', the latter being 'the epithet given to a substance with a tendency to vaporize and rise upward'[11]—in short, as spirit. Thus alchemy itself also constitutes a double-realm.

To return to Ruland's definition of meditation as 'an internal talk of one person with another who is invisible': strangely enough—or maybe not so strangely—this is reminiscent of the young Goethe's practice of apparently holding actual conversation with the characters of his imagination, this having begun in 1769 and early 1770 after a serious breakdown in health while studying at Leipzig and before his departure for Strasburg. It was also during this period that, through a friend of his mother's, the Pietist Susanne von Klettenberg, he first really became acquainted with alchemy. With her he began a study

---

8. Appropriately, this takes place offstage; but the essential information about this domain and its ruling spirits is provided by Mephistopheles in the *Dark Gallery* scene (Norton, pp. 155–9, and HA, pp. 190–94).

9. Indeed, there is a reference to the *laterna magica* in the scene of the carnival masque at the Emperor's court, Part 2, Act 1 (Norton, p. 140; HA, lines 5516–18, p. 172). For a detailed explanatory note on this, see the commentary by Albrecht Schöne in *Goethe Faust* (Deutscher Klassiker, 1994), pp. 479–84.

10. Rilke, *Die Sonette an Orpheus*, Part 1, No. 9, in *Sämtliche Werke* 1 (Insel-Verlag 1962), p. 736.

11. See Lyndy Abraham, *A Dictionary of Alchemical Imagery* (Cambridge, 1998), p. 212.

of Paracelsus and read Georg von Welling's vast compilation, *Opus Mago-Cabbalisticum et Theosophicum* (1735), and the anonymous *Aurea Catena Homeri* (1723), later attributed to Joseph Kirchweger; both were printed at Frankfurt, which was still a centre of alchemy as it had been since the sixteenth century. Goethe also records that his illness (which seems to have been tubercular neck-glands) was treated at this time by Dr J. F. Metz, whose application of a phial of alchemical crystallized salt led to his complete recovery. Impressed by this, the young student set up his own laboratory in the attic at home and began seriously to experiment. Consequently in a letter of 26 August 1770, after his move to Strasburg, he could write to Fräulein von Klettenberg: 'Yet alchemy is still my veiled Love'; and later, in his autobiography *Dichtung und Wahrheit* (*Poetry and Truth*), he could say of his meeting with Herder in the same city:

> But, most of all, I concealed from Herder my mystico-cabbalistical chemistry, and every thing relating to it; although at the same time, I was still very fond of secretly busying myself in working it out more consistently than it had been communicated to me.[12]

Goethe's characteristic thoroughness in mining a field of knowledge that preoccupied him emerges forcefully here; and we can assume that not only were his studies in alchemy, like those of Faust himself, significantly broad and deep, as we shall see later, but also that they had begun to permeate his ways of thought and *Weltanschauung*. For the moment it is enough to note this statement in a letter to his Leipzig friend, Ernst Theodor Langer, just after his recovery at the hands of Dr Metz: 'Much has happened to me; I have struggled and am free, this calcination was needed in my soul'.[13] Alchemical and soul-processes are hereby fused together early on in the poet's career; the calcinations being the reduction through fiery

12. Translation by John Oxenford (1882); see *The Autobiography of Johann Wolfgang von Goethe* (Sidgwick and Jackson, 1971), vol. 2, p. 22. German text in HA 9, p. 414.
13. Translated by Alice Raphael in her *Goethe and the Philosophers' Stone* (Routledge, 1965), pp. 15–16.

heat of a metal or mineral to powder or dust, so that, as Lyndy Abraham puts it in her *Dictionary of Alchemical Imagery*, 'the metallic body (or soul of man)' is reduced 'into its first matter and renders it porous so that it may more easily receive the influx of the divine tincture or spirit'.[14] In the young Goethe's case an analogy is clearly being made to the fiery course of his illness, the entailed suffering necessary for his continued wellbeing, and his resulting recovery. Thus alchemy made a decisively personal inroad into the poet's early life, quite apart from his intellectual interest in the subject. So much so that his entire life-pattern, which he categorized as '*eine wiederholte Pubertät*' ('a repeated puberty'),[15] involving emotional crisis, illness, and recovery, can be said to mirror and enact the actual alchemical process of *solve et coagula* (dissolve and coagulate), something which can be equally well applied to the poet's *alter ego*, Faust.

Further evidence of the linkage here suggested is provided by Goethe's advice in 1770 to a younger Frankfurt contemporary just about to embark on his university studies—namely, that 'we must not seek to *be* anything but to *become* everything'[16]—and we can compare this with what Faust says to Mephistopheles straight after their wager and pact:

> Mein Busen, der von Wissensdrang geheilt ist,
> Soll keinen Schmerzen künftig sich verschliessen,
> Und was der ganzen Menschheit zugeteilt ist,
> Will ich in meinen innern Selbst geniessen,
> Mit meinem Geist das Höchst' und Tiefste greifen,
> Ihr Wohl und Weh auf meinen Busen häufen,
> Und so mein eigen Selbst zu ihrem Selbst erweitern,
> Und, wie sie selbst, am End' auch ich zerscheitern.

14. Abraham, *A Dictionary of Alchemical Imagery*, p. 31.
15. See the passage from 11 March 1828 in *Conversations of Goethe with Eckermann*, trans. John Oxenford (Bell, 1913), p. 16.
16. Quoted by Nicholas Boyle in *Goethe (The Poet and the Age)*, vol. 1: *The Poetry of Desire (1749–1790)* (Oxford, 1992), p. 91.

My heart, from learning's tyranny set free,
Shall no more shun distress, but take its toll,
Of all the hazards of humanity,
And nourish mortal sadness in my soul.
I'll sound the heights and depths that men can know,
Their very souls shall be with mine entwined,
I'll load my bosom with their weal and woe,
And share with them the shipwreck of mankind.[17]

In the poet's advice to his fellow student emphasis is placed on an expansively encompassing sense of self; similarly in the *Faust* passage what is stressed is its hero's desire to experience 'the heights and depths that men can know', 'their weal and woe', *Und so mein eigen Selbst zu ihrem Selbst erweitern*, more exactly translated as 'And thereby expand my own self to include their own'. In both cases the movement of thought is alike; although in the *Faust* extract it is important to realize that now that Faust is 'from learning's tyranny set free', he is interested in a very different kind of knowledge, which is only to be acquired by stepping out of his scholar's Gothic study into a whole new world of experience—human, feminine, social, including that of nature and the cosmos—in fact, just what Mephisto can provide him with. For the two of them then travel through time and space, Faust's encounters in the course of this transmuting into a knowledge that has nothing to do with books and the learning of the schools, matters of intellect, or the accumulation of facts, but with life itself, the heart and its emotions, sensory exploration and enjoyment, the exercise of magical powers, and a quest for feminine beauty. Tragedies, of course, are inevitable along this path.

Initially, however, as in the great *Forest and Cavern* scene of Part I, what Faust experiences is a new and total immersion both in wild nature and the domain of 'my inner self' (*meinem innern Selbst*), his meeting and relationship with Gretchen having already begun to transform his inner metabolism. His magnificent soliloquy there,

---

17. HA, p. 59, lines 1768–75 (p. 48); Payne, pp. 89–90.

with its exalted address to the Earth-Spirit, records these newly received gifts of experience, at the same time presenting them as complementary fields: freshly discovered nature (the macrocosm) and his inner self (the microcosm). In fact, the scene's very title points to this, the forest embodying nature's universe—'*Gabst mir die herrliche Natur zum Königreich*' ('You gave me glorious nature for a kingdom'); the cavern, to which he retreats during a storm, being the spot where the inner self is opened up: '*Dann führst du mich zur sichern Höhle, zeigst/Mich dann mir selbst, und meiner eignen Brust/Geheime tiefe Wunder öffnen sich*' ('You lead my steps within the sheltering cavern/ Where I may meet my soul, and all the heart/Of wonder in my spirit stands revealed').[18] Thus outer and inner are brought together as in philosophical alchemy. And it is therefore not coincidental that Faust says to the Earth-Spirit with reference to nature: '*Vergönnest mir, in ihre tiefe Brust,/Wie in den Busen eines Freunds, zu schauen*' ('You taught me in her deepest heart to gaze,/To seek as in the bosom of a friend'), where nature's 'deepest heart' (literally, 'her deep breast') is not only linked to the friend's bosom but to Faust himself in the cavern. *Brust/Busen* are used three times to unify the whole soliloquy, macrocosm with microcosm, while the natural world is depicted as a realm to be felt intimately, not encountered in cold detachment.

Hence nature and the cosmos are now taken up into Faust's responsive subjectivity, and we find ourselves in a world close to that of Wordsworth's *Tintern Abbey*. So that if we then maintain that this ushers us into an early Romantic universe—in Goethe's case one of *Sturm und Drang* ('Storm and Stress')—we can see that the *Forest and Cavern* monologue, in its fusion of the experience of wild nature with its emotionally inward reception, and especially in constituting a new form of knowledge, is very much of the essence of Goethe's and Wordsworth's period. Most visibly at this point in the drama, but elsewhere, too, and more substantially in Part I than in the more classical Part II, a *Sturm und Drang* Faust joins hands with a more historical Faust of late medieval–early Renaissance times.

18. HA, p. 103, lines 3232–4; Payne, p. 145.

Indeed, there is a close connection (often unnoticed because of the late seventeenth- and eighteenth-century upsurge of natural science and Enlightenment thinking which came between) that links Renaissance alchemy and hermeticism with the new Romantic concepts of nature and the self. Goethe and his contemporaries, we know, found great sustenance in thinkers such as Giordano Bruno, Ficino, and Pico della Mirandola; as also in Cornelius Agrippa, from whom Goethe took his idea for the apparition of Mephisto as a black poodle;[19] and again in Jakob Boehme, whose work is steeped in alchemical thought-forms, thereby building a bridge between the Renaissance thinkers and later Protestant mysticism. One can certainly argue that Boehme was responsible for starting to 'psychologize' alchemy in a Pietistic manner, and that both Goethe and Jung picked up this thread. However, note first of all the following account of Renaissance hermeticism from M. H. Abrams's *Natural Supernaturalism*:

Renaissance vitalism had envisioned an integral universe without absolute divisions, in which everything is interrelated by a system of correspondences, and the living is continuous with the inanimate, nature with man, and matter with mind; a universe, moreover, which is activated throughout by a dynamism of opposing forces which not only sustains its present existence but also keeps it moving along the way back toward the unity of its origin. In this way of thinking some Romantic philosophers detected intimations of a viable counter-metaphysic to contemporary mechanism, elementarism, and dualism; provided that (as Schelling said with respect to Boehme . . .) the mythical elements are translated into philosophical concepts, and these are ordered into a 'scientific', that is, a coherent conceptual system.[20]

This picture of 'an integral universe without absolute divisions, in which everything is interrelated by a system of correspondences' is

---

19. See *HA*, pp. 41–2, lines 1147–73; Payne, pp. 68–9.
20. M. H. Abrams, *Natural Supernaturalism* (Norton, 1973), p. 171.

very much Faust's own world, since the operation of magic is viable only where man as microcosm is deeply mirrored in nature as macrocosm, both being underpinned by a connecting and encompassing *anima mundi* structured as a spiritual hierarchy. Ascending and descending levels are thereby interlinked, as in the traditional concept of the Chain of Being, so that the magus, through the power of his art, can summon from up or down the great staircase the spiritual beings inhabiting these levels. In Faust's own case we get in the play's opening his nocturnal invocation through Nostradamus of 'the sign of the macrocosm' with its rejuvenating influx,[21] closely followed by the Earth-Spirit's terrifying presence in his spurt of flame.[22] Later, outside the city walls, when returning with his disciple Wagner from their Easter walk, Faust invokes almost without realizing what he is doing those 'aerial spirits'[23] about whom Wagner, the humanist pedant, rightly warns his master, and as a result of which Mephistopheles soon appears out of the evening mists in the shape of the famous black poodle.

At this juncture it is worth briefly mentioning Harold Jantz's valuable study, *Goethe's Faust as a Renaissance Man*, which reminds us of the Renaissance's wide-spectrum attitude to the supernatural, in which every shade and gradation were allowed for, especially those of the so-called 'middle spirits' whom Paracelsus terms 'elemental beings'. For as Jantz makes clear: 'In the Renaissance the more freely speculative writers combined the pagan elf and fairy lore of their own lands with the spirit lore of Graeco-Roman antiquity.'[24] And there is much of this syncretism in *Faust*, as witness the parallel scenes of the *Walpurgisnacht* and the *Klassische Walpurgisnacht* (also the *Walpurgisnachtstraum* or *Oberon's and Titania's Golden Wedding*)—which reminds us of Goethe's love of Shakespeare's *A Midsummer Night's Dream* and *The Tempest*, and of Ovid's *Metamorphoses*. Finally here, with M. H. Abrams's 'integral universe without absolute divisions' in

21. HA, pp. 21–3, lines 418–59; Payne, pp. 45–6.
22. HA, pp. 23–4, lines 460–515; Payne, pp. 46–8.
23. HA, p. 41, lines 1118–41; Payne, pp. 67–8.
24. Harold Jantz: *Goethe's Faust as a Renaissance Man* (Princeton, 1951), p. 28.

mind, one can further argue that the very structure of *Faust* with its different yet interconnecting imaginative levels and scene locations is an exact mirror image of this statement.

For again, the drama's overall forms and its hero's career are essentially open not closed, Goethe's use of what is called the scrapbook (*Fetzenscenen*) technique, which the *Sturm und Drang* playwrights adapted for their own purpose from their study of Shakespeare, accounting for this structurally. Basically, it meant cutting from scene to scene and rapidly changing the place of action without any linkage, as in a magic lantern or film show. This is especially true of Part I, which has no act divisions or even numbering of scenes; while in the more classical Part II with its characteristic five acts the same principle is fundamentally at work, with unexpected shifts of scene still operating, although the pace of the action is now more leisurely. Furthermore, Goethe's drama does not actually begin with Faust's long opening monologue in his study at night, but with the two introductory stage events prefacing this: the *Prelude on the Stage* and the *Prologue in Heaven*. The former, as we saw in the last chapter, was modelled on the *Prologue* to Kalidasa's play *Shakuntala*, which Goethe had read with great excitement in 1791; the latter on the opening to *The Book of Job*, where Satan appears among 'the sons of God' to converse with the Lord. The theme of 'Hast thou considered my servant Job?' is transposed as:

DER HERR Kennst du den Faust?
MEPHISTOPHELES   Den Doktor?
DER HERR   Meinen Knecht!

THE LORD *Know you one Faust?*
MEPHISTOPHELES   *The Doctor?*
THE LORD   *Him, my servant.*[25]

This exchange, plus their wager on whether such a servant can be seduced away from God or not, means that thematically Faust

25. *HA*, p. 17, line 229; Payne, p. 40.

precedes his own entry into the drama. And as if to reinforce this, his opening soliloquy begins *in media res*:

Habe nun, ach! Philosophie,
Juristerei und Medizin,
Und leider auch Theologie
Durchaus studiert, mit heissem Bemühn.[26]

Have now, alas! thoroughly studied
Philosophy, jurisprudence, medicine,
And, sorry to say, theology, too,
With fervour and substantial pains.[27]

The upshot is that this scene is thereby tied into and somehow ongoing from the *Prologue in Heaven*, with the celestial domain and its diabolic presence seen to be clearly in touch with the earthly, even if there is a definite sense throughout the play that humankind very much inhabits its own special terrain. Nevertheless, bear in mind that in Part II's final episode we re-ascend to a heavenly, albeit different, level with Faust's post-mortem self. The stage directions are marked 'Mountain Ravines: Forest, Rock, Desert. Holy anchorites scattered upon the mountainside, secluded in rocky clefts',[28] where the topography like the action leads upward. We get other stage directions in between, such as 'tiefe Region', 'mittlere Region', and so on, relating to the anchorites' various positions, then a 'Choir of Blissful Boys circling around the highest peaks', followed by 'Angels hovering in the upper atmosphere carrying Faust's immortal part', with Doctor Marianus, holiest of the anchorites, stationed 'in the highest, purest cell'—an ironically backward glance, surely, to Faust's gloomy and very different study, where the drama opens. The last section of this final scene also ushers in mainly feminine figures, among them the transfigured Gretchen, Faust's great early love, as Una Poenitentium

---

26. *HA*, p. 20, lines 354–7.
27. My translation, which tries to bring out this sense of *in medias res*.
28. My translation; cf. Norton, p. 300; *HA*, p. 356.

and the Mater Gloriosa herself, who calls on the former to 'Come! Lift yourself to higher spheres!' Thus as spectators we find ourselves re-entering the world of the *Prologue in Heaven*, having travelled along a vast irregular circle; only this time, instead of the three archangels Raphael, Gabriel, and Michael, plus the Lord and Mephistopheles, we encounter a panoply of feminine beings culminating in the play's famous last two lines: '*Das Ewig-Weibliche/Zieht uns hinan*' ('The Eternal-Feminine/Draws us upward').[29] So that the masculine *Prologue* is complemented by the feminine close in what one might see as an alchemical balancing out and retrospective fusion—in short, a 'chymical wedding', if of a very ethereal kind. Moreover, we have experienced an overall cyclical movement from start to finish, beginning and ending beyond the confines of the physical world, something which would appear to mirror the *opus circulatorium* itself, another name for the *opus alchymicum*. To quote Johannes Fabricius on this:

> The circular path of the sun through the Zodiac is the model of the *opus alchymicum*, which is frequently called the *opus circulatorium* . . . All-important is the dualistic view of the universe as the battleground of opposing forces. The alchemists' intention is to resolve this conflict harmoniously (1) by a 'putrefying' movement of death and rebirth, (2) by a return to the primal matter; and (3) by a rotatory movement turning the wheel of creation backward in an *opus contra naturam* aimed at a return to the source of all creation, or 'God'. This is the famed opus circulatorium, in which the subject of regeneration consumes himself in the manner of the uroboric serpent.[30]

The above passage charts in alchemical terms, I believe, both the general shape of Goethe's play as well as Faust's own career, so that the work itself becomes the *opus alchymicum*, its hero's path through life and beyond embodying the alchemical process and changes *en route*. Emphasis is also laid here on hermetic science's desire to

29. *HA*, p. 364, lines 12110–11; my translation; cf. Norton, p. 308.
30. Fabricius, pp. 15 and 17.

resolve harmoniously all dualistic views of life, which is Goethe's own position both in *Faust* and in his anti-Newtonian *Farbenlehre* (*Theory of Colours*).[31]

Now, more specifically, one can relate the first stage in the alchemical process detailed above—namely, 'a "putrefying" movement of death and rebirth'—to Faust's initial situation in his night-time study, which culminates in thoughts of suicide as he lifts the poisoned chalice once belonging to his father to his lips, yet just when the sound of Easter bells and church choir begin to celebrate Christ's Resurrection, so that overwhelming feelings of rebirth make him desist. Clearly he has gone through a dark night of the soul, something which can be seen as embodying the initial phase of the alchemical process, the *nigredo*, a blackening disintegrating state, of which the *putrefactio* is part. As Lyndy Abraham puts it, this is

> the initial, black stage of the opus alchymicum in which the body of the impure metal, the matter for the Stone, or the old outmoded state of being is killed, putrefied and dissolved into the original substance of creation, the *prima materia*, in order that it may be renovated and reborn in a new form.[32]

This also includes Johannes Fabricius's second point, 'a return to the primal matter', as well as heralding his third, 'a rotatory movement

---

31. As Henri Bortoft puts it in the Preface to *Goethe on Science* (an anthology of Goethe's scientific writings), selected and introduced by Jeremy Naydler (Floris Books, 1996):

Goethe did not subscribe to the dualism of the two-world theory, with its notion of the archetype as 'one over many' which is separate from the multiplicity of particular phenomena. The whole of his scientific work was in the opposite direction to this kind of metaphysical dualism. . . . But this is far from being a naive empiricism, which sees the surface appearance as all there is to the phenomenon' (p. 11).

Consult, too, Bortoft's splendid full-length study, *The Wholeness of Nature (Goethe's Way of Science)* (Floris Books, 1996).

32. Abraham, *A Dictionary of Alchemical Imagery*, p. 135.

turning the wheel of creation backward in an *opus contra naturam* aimed at a return to the source of all creation, or God', since through the church bells and choir this is exactly what happens. Faust immediately goes back in his memory to the springtime of his youth before all his problems of epistemology and ontology have begun. As he exclaims: '*O tönet fort, ihr süssen Himmelslieder!/Die Träne quillt, die Erde hat mich wieder!*' ('Begin once more, O sweet celestial strain!/ Tears dim my eyes: earth's child I am again').[33] So what we discover in this highly complex, inwardly fluctuating scene is a miniature *opus circulatorium* that structurally and psychologically sets the pattern for the entire drama. Faust's initial rebirth, too, as already stated, is significantly inaugurated at just the crucial moment when Christ's Resurrection is being solemnized, an alchemical event of supreme importance in that Christ Himself in medieval alchemy—the risen Christ, that is—was looked upon as being the philosophers' stone itself, the *lapis philosophorum*, something which would seem to be indicated by the scene's last choral stanza: '*Christ ist erstanden,/Aus der Verwesung Schoss*' ('Christ has arisen/Out of putrefaction's womb!').[34]

I should now like to consider the consciously corresponding scene which opens Part II, where Faust likewise undergoes another rebirth preceded by a similar, if differing state of disintegration that takes place, however, in the final episode of Part I set in Gretchen's prison cell. This is another *nigredo* situation, more dramatic and violent this time, where Gretchen, awaiting her death sentence for killing her child by Faust and already half demented, refuses to be saved by the diabolical means offered her. Faust himself is heart-stricken with remorse: 'Would that I had never been born!'; but is whipped away by Mephisto and appears only half awake, yet restless and unable to find sleep, although it is dusk. The scene is marked *Anmutige Gegend* (*Charming Locality*), and it possesses quasi-Elysian overtones.[35]

During its first half, Ariel and a chorus of nature-spirits hold

33. *HA*, p. 31, lines 783–4; Payne, p. 56.
34. *HA*, p. 32, lines 797–8; cf. Payne, p. 57, but my translation here.
35. *HA*, pp. 146–9; Norton, pp. 118–21.

consultation on Faust's condition and new surroundings. The former, to the sound of Aolian harps, commands the latter to assist him, as they do in the shape of elves each spring both for 'the just and the unjust'. In this case it means bathing the guilty man 'in dew from Lethe's flood' so that, salved in forgetfulness, he can be given back to 'the holy light', something which takes place in the second half of the scene. Lethe, as we know, is the river of forgetting the past in the Greek underworld; but here Goethe has Dante more in mind, where Lethe flows not in hell but in the earthly paradise (*Purgatorio*, Canto 28) and souls, admittedly penitent, are purged and purified. To point up this context, Faust's great monologue on awakening—'*Des Lebens Pulse schlagen frisch lebendig*' ('Life's pulses now are beating afresh')— is written in *terza rima*.[36] But it is not printed as such, being set up in roughly fifty lines of irregular verse paragraphs, so that it is more a soliloquy marking a decisive change of inner direction on its hero's part. Nevertheless, a small Dantesque pilgrimage is sketched in, spaced out in four stages; and this precisely echoes Ariel's line spoken earlier about nature's period of rest between evening and morning twilight: '*VIER sind die Pausen nächtiger Weile*' ('*FOUR* are the watches marking night-time's passing').[37] During this period the nature-spirits will extract '*des Vorwurfs glühend bittre Pfeile*' ('self-reproach's arrows of bitter fire') and purify '*sein Innres . . . von erlebtem Graus*' ('his heart . . . of lived-through horror'). The four watches are then described in four separate stanzas comprising as follows: (i) twilight's descent with accompanying sleep; (ii) the coming of night with 'star after star' and 'the moon's full splendour'; (iii) a period of suspended time when 'pain and happiness' both evaporate and '[one] becomes hale' again as the shapes of valley and hill, bushes with their shadows, and silvery waves of unripe grain begin to emerge; and (iv) when it is time to throw off 'sleep's husk' and start the new day's activity.

Thus we note how inner and outer are here brought together, Faust's stages of recovery and rebirth bearing an exact parallel to the

---

36. *HA*, pp. 148–9, lines 4679–727; Norton, pp. 120–21, but my translation here.
37. Norton, p. 118, but my translation; *HA*, p. 146, line 4626.

diurnal round of the macrocosm. This is possible, I believe, only by virtue of 'the alchemical substructure underpinning this scene. To begin with, one perceives the emphasis on inner and outer transformation and the fact that, as with the overall alchemical process itself, there are four major stages traditionally described in terms of colour: the *nigredo* (black); the *albedo* (white); the *citrinitas* (lemon); and the *rubedo* (ruby red). The first stage, that of the *nigredo*, is easy to locate in Faust's inner state of bitter self-reproach, with its roots in the Gretchen prison scene, which is exactly the frame of mind and heart he is in as evening twilight descends, so that with it the process of *purificatio* can begin. The second major stage of healing or 'whitening', the *albedo*, is—for our purpose here—revealingly detailed by Johannes Fabricius:

In the albedo the *virgin* and the *moon* appear as the great alchemical symbols of sublimation. The polluted soul extracted and purified in heaven gradually acquires the features of the heavenly Virgin, just as the perilous new moon by means of ablution is transformed into the glittering half-moon, then into the three-quarters phase and finally into the full moon of the 'white' rebirth.[38]

At which we should recall from the nature-spirits' second stanza the appropriate lines: '*Tiefsten Ruhens Glück besiegelnd/Herrscht des Mondes volle Pracht*' ('Sealing happiness's deepest peace / There reigns the moon's full splendour'). The third stage, that of the *citrinitas*, becomes the yellowing dawn ushered in with the spirits' third stanza; and Lyndy Abraham is here relevant:

The clear moonlight of the albedo leads the adept out of the black night of the soul (the nigredo) into the dawning of consciousness, (i.e. the *citrinitas*), heralding the advent of full consciousness symbolized by the midday sun at the final red stage of the opus, the rubedo.[39]

---

38. Fabricius, *Alchemy*, p. 111.
39. Abraham, *A Dictionary of Alchemical Imagery*, p. 5.

This fourth stage is only indirectly accentuated in the spirits' fourth stanza, since it is Ariel himself, coming straight after and initiating the full violence and explosion of the new day, who really introduces this phase of the process, before it is taken up in its total splendour by the awakening Faust.

The monologue which ensues, as indicated above, is a linchpin in terms of the protagonist's inner development and new orientation towards nature and the cosmos. These can be initially portrayed as, first of all, a restructuring or, at the least, modification of Faustian 'striving' (*streben*), forced on him by his confronting the full glare of the rising sun—a physical impossibility highly reminiscent of his earlier inability to face the Earth-Spirit in the opening scene to Part I. Secondly, a more appreciative, more aesthetic, hence quasi-classical awareness of nature takes place on his recovery in the midst of such Elysian surroundings. The new release of feeling is less ecstatic, however, if more considered and considering, than that embodied in his *Forest and Cavern* soliloquy.

To take the second first, since this is the theme of the opening verse-paragraph. There Faust shows a new consciousness of the role played by the earth in his recovery. Greeting the morning twilight, he exclaims: '*Du, Erde, warst auch diese Nacht beständig/Und atmest neu erquickt zu meinen Füssen,/Beginnest schon, mit Lust mich zu umgeben*' ('You, Earth, were also steadfast through this night/And breathe now at my feet rejuvenated afresh,/Already beginning to surround me with pleasure'). But this address momentarily results in the stirring up of his old desires: '*Zum höchsten Dasein immerfort zu streben*' ('To strive continually for the highest being'), although he then resumes the delighted notation of his immediate environment: the hundreds of birdcalls echoing out of the woods, the swathes of early morning mist in the valleys, the freeing of scents and colours, and flowers and leafage dripping with dew; so that he can finally proclaim: '*Ein Paradies wird um mich her die Runde*' ('A paradise lies circled round about me'). Again, another allusion to Dante—this time to his Earthly Paradise. Then, after Faust has continued his response to the landscape by gazing up towards the most distant mountains and recording the stepwise descent of the first light upon their slopes, a passage in which Goethe is recalling a memorable journey he made through Switzerland in 1797, we reach the point where the sun appears and blinds him: '*Sie tritt hervor!—und leider schon geblendet,/Kehr' ich mich weg, vom Augenschmerz durchdrungen*' ('He steps forth, and already unfortunately dazzled/I turn away, pierced by the pain in my eyes'). He next applies this situation to man's inner life—his longings and hopes—significantly switching from 'I' to 'we', so that Faust is generalizing from his own position outwards. For just as with the rising sun we gaze and wait in expectation for it to burst over the horizon, so with our hopes and longings, as they hover on the brink of fulfilment, a surplus of possibilities overwhelms us, creating like the sun 'an excess of flame', 'a sea of fire', with the result that we likewise turn away back to earth, surrounded '*Mit Schmerz und Freuden wechselnd ungeheuer*' ('With pain and joy monstrously alternating'). The imagery here suggests the so-called 'reddening stage of the opus', with the alternating 'pain and joy' indicative of a *coniunctio oppositorum*, that conjunction of opposites marking the goal of Hermetic science. Indeed, the risen sun in all its majesty is used to symbolize the philosophers' stone itself, as beautifully portrayed in the final picture of the *Splendor Solis* series (1582) of Salomon Trismosin. But Faust is unable to do anything with this, opting instead, as we shall see in a moment, for the waterfall and its rainbow. Firstly, though, it is worth underscoring the connection between his monologue in this scene and those already mentioned from Part I—where the Earth-Spirit is directly invoked in his scholar's study, then its unnamed presence indirectly addressed in *Forest and Cavern*.[40] For here, in the opening to Part II, its invisible hand is clearly at work in the activity of Ariel and his attendant spirits. Its presence, yet at the same time invisibility, while providing Goethe with the right connective tissue, marks a subtle shift in perspective characteristic of Part II as a whole—namely, a retreat behind the scenes of the Paracelsian

40. Cf. Payne, pp. 46–8 with p. 145; and *HA*, pp. 23–4, lines 460–517, with p. 103, lines 3217–24.

spirit of nature in favour of a lighter, more distanced agent. As with the drama's key-motif of striving, which keeps on resurfacing through-out, these manifestations of the Earth-Spirit are an instance of what Harold Jantz has termed 'echo structures', which he sees as one of the play's organizing formal principles.[41]

But to return. Faust now places the sun behind him—'So then, let the sun remain behind me'—and directs his attention instead to the waterfall rushing down through its ridge of rock (*Der Wassersturz, das Felsenriff durchbrausend*) 'with growing rapture' and especially the rainbow spanning its descent, which he turns into a new and power-ful symbol with which to re-orientate himself:

> *DER* spiegelt ab das menschliche Bestreben,
> Ihm sinne nach, und du begreifst genauer:
> Am farbigen Abglanz haben wir das Leben.

> *IT mirrors human striving: reflect on this,*
> *And you will understand more clearly:*
> *From images of colour we take our life.*[42]

In these lines, as in the verse-paragraph immediately preceding, we get a very different definition of, and location for, human striving, one that not only centres it in life and nature as opposed to the beyond—for such lies above our capacities—but also that human endeavour and its goals—the essences and truths which man is always climbing after—must now be mediated and filtered through their images, reflections and symbols here on earth. With these three verses a new stage in Faust's inner development is reached cognate with Goethe's own beliefs. In fact, the way these lines are expressed gives them a definite authorial ring, since they embody a newly dis-covered insight, reflective advice, and a philosophical summation of

---

41. See Harold Jantz, *The Form of 'Faust'* (Johns Hopkins University Press, 1978), pp. 120–21.

42. *HA*, p. 149, lines 4725–7; Norton, p. 121, but my translation.

where we are or should be—something disclosed through Faust's switching again from an 'I' to a 'you' and 'we' position in this last section of his speech. Indeed, Goethe formulated a comparable statement to all this in the introduction to his 1825 *Essay on a Theory of the Weather*, addressed to the English meteorologist Luke Howard, with whom he was conducting an exchange of letters:

Das Wahre mit dem Göttlichen identisch, lässt sich niemals von uns direct erkennen, wir schauen es nur im Abglanz, im Beispiel, Symbol, in einzelnen und verwandten Erscheinungen; wir werden es gewahr als unbegreifliches Leben und können dem Wunsch nicht entsagen, es dennoch zu begreifen. Dieses gilt von allen Phänomenen der fasslichen Welt.

The truth, which is identical with the divine, will never be directly perceived by us. We can only behold it via images, examples, symbols, and in single, related appearances. We will become aware of it as incomprehensible life and yet will not be able to renounce the wish to comprehend it. This is true of all the phenomena of the intelligible world.[43]

Note that the same word, *Abglanz* (image/reflection), is used in both extracts. It is a favourite of Goethe's, being the title of one of his *West-Östlicher Divan* poems[44] as well as a term from his *Theory of Colours*. The rainbow's *farbiger Abglanz* also possesses alchemical overtones related to the image of the *cauda pavonis* or 'peacock's tail', as witness the following:

When the blackness of the *nigredo* is washed away, it is succeeded by the appearance of all the colours of the rainbow, which look like a peacock displaying its luminescent tail. Jung has suggested that

43. German text in *HA*, 13, p. 305; my translation. Consult, too, Albrecht Schöne's commentary (see n. 9 above), pp. 410–12.
44. See *HA* 2, p. 86.

the basis for this phenomenon may be the iridescent skin that often forms on the surface of molten metal.[45]

Now Faust's progress along the curve of self-knowledge and self-development, in spite of various backslidings and sidetrackings (what Jung terms 'the individuation process' and which he sees embodied in 'philosophical alchemy'), cannot, for Goethe, exclude constant involvement with the so-called 'real world' outside the self. As he formulated it in 1823: 'Man can only know himself in so far as he himself is within the world'.[46] Thus his position here comprises what might be described as a form of dialectical holism, in which reciprocal interconnections are seen as mutually determining, yet where outside realities can only be known by man 'within himself'. For the poet, as indeed for Faust, a crucial emphasis on individuating processes of inner change and development, where matters of self-perception, self-understanding, and self-growth are of the essence, is of major concern, being at the heart of their speculations on the nature and destiny of man. Such speculations, of course, possess their own specific philosophical history and in this case have roots going back to medieval scholasticism's concept of the *principium individuationis*, itself deriving from Aristotle, in which the law responsible for creating individual human uniqueness (Jung's 'individual differentiation') was epitomized.[47] The source and nature of this law were heatedly debated by medieval philosophers from Albertus Magnus and Thomas Aquinas to Duns Scotus, Meister Eckhart, and Nikolaus Cusanus; then to resurface actively and self-consciously in the work of Leibniz, Kant, Fichte, and others.[48] Goethe would have been familiar with much of this, firstly via Leibniz's more dynamic usage of the scholastic term, secondly, in that it was closely identical with the Aristotelian concept of entelechy which,

45. Abraham, *A Dictionary of Alchemical Imagery*, pp. 141–2.
46. See HA 13 (*Naturwissenschaftliche Schriften* 1), trans. Karl Viëtor, p. 38.
47. See *De Anima*, trans. J. A. Smith, in *The Works of Aristotle*, vol. III, ed. W. D. Ross (Oxford, 1931), pp. 402–35.
48. Consult Jolande Jacobi, *The Way of Individuation* (Hodder and Stoughton, 1967), p. 13, and especially n. 3 to that page, pp. 144–5.

as we shall directly see, was incorporated into the thinking and text of *Faust*.

For in Part II's final scene, where the stage directions announce their hero's apotheosis with '*Angels* hovering in the upper atmosphere, bearing Faust's immortal part', we know that the dramatist's original draft for this was 'Choir of Angels, above the mountaintop, bringing up Faust's entelechy'.[49] Like the Leibnizian monad, this is indestructible and what survives death. In his *Conversations with Eckermann* we find several references to the idea of entelechy which are worth introducing at this juncture. On 1 September 1829, for instance, just three years before Goethe died, we get this: 'I doubt not of our immortality, for nature cannot dispense with the *entelecheia*.'[50] And again on 3 March 1830: 'Leibniz had similar thoughts about independent beings, and indeed what we term an *entelecheia* he calls a monad.'[51] But the most substantial and revealing passage comes from 11 March 1828:

Every *Entelechia* [*sic*] is a piece of eternity, and the few years during which it is bound to the earthly body does not make it old . . . But if the *Entelechia* [*sic*] is of a powerful kind, as is the case with all men of natural genius, then with its animating penetration of the body it will not only act with strengthening and ennobling power upon the organisation, but it will also endeavour with its spiritual superiority to confer the privilege of perpetual youth. Thence it comes that in men of superior endowments, even during their old age, we constantly perceive fresh epochs of singular productiveness; they seem constantly to grow young again for a time, and that is what I call a repeated puberty [*wiederholte Pubertät*].[52]

As we said earlier, this 'repeated puberty' mirrors the alchemical

---

49. Norton, p. 303, but my translation. Also consult Erich Trunz's commentary in HA, pp. 627–33.

50. Quoted in Raphael, *Goethe and the Philosophers' Stone*, p. 247.

51. Ibid.

52. Ibid. This and the two previous quotes trans. John Oxenford (1913).

process of *solve et coagula*,[53] so that Faust's entelechy and its further upward progress as detailed by the various groups of Angels and Blessed Boys are thereby alchemicized. For as Alice Raphael has pointed out in her *Goethe and the Philosophers' Stone*, 'alchemical references now begin to creep into the final scene'.[54] For example: after the Younger Angels have referred to the impact made in the previous *Grablegung* (*Burial*) scene, where they pelt Mephistopheles with roses of heavenly fire in order to burn and distract him, so that Faust's 'immortal part' can be surreptitiously borne aloft, they say of these same flowers that they

> Halfen uns den Sieg gewinnen,
> Uns das hohe Werk vollenden,
> Diesen Seelenschatz erbeuten.

> *Helped us win this victory,*
> *Helped us complete the noble work,*
> *And capture this soul's treasure.*[55]

'The noble work' (*das hohe Werk*), an expression often used in alchemy to designate the final *opus*, also seems indicated here, where both individuating and alchemical processes have now coalesced; especially when taken in conjunction with 'this soul's treasure', a phrase completely in line with 'the spiritual conversion of man' viewed by the alchemists 'as analogous to the purification of metals'.[56] Again, the More Perfect Angels continue this flow of thought with

> Uns bleibt ein Erdenrest
> Zu tragen peinlich,
> Und wär' er von Asbest,
> Er ist nicht reinlich.

53. See above, p. 48.
54. Raphael, *Goethe and the Philosophers' Stone*, p. 227.
55. *HA*, p. 359, lines 11944–6; Norton, p. 303, but my translation.
56. Abraham, *A Dictionary of Alchemical Imagery*, p. 46.

An earthly fragment still remains
For us to carry painfully,
Yet even if made of asbestos,
It would not be pure.[57]

Asbestos, I take it, is postulated since it is a silicate mineral resistant to fire and therefore would remain essentially untouched after undergoing the heats of purification. Nevertheless, for all its qualities of survival, still not really pure enough. The More Perfect Angels then continue with this central passage:

Wenn starke Geisteskraft
Die Elemente
An sich herangerafft,
Kein Engel trennte
Geeinte Zwienatur
Der innigen beiden,
Die ewige Liebe nur
Vermag's zu scheiden.

When strong force of spirit
Has gathered the elements
To itself, no angel can separate
The unified double-nature
Of its two inner qualities:
Only eternal love is able
To separate these quite.[58]

These lines have been interpreted as giving expression to Goethe's theory of incarnation and reincarnation, during the course of which man's existence is seen as a 'unified double-nature',[59] something that

57. Norton, p. 303, but my translation; *HA*, p. 359, lines 11954–7.
58. Norton, pp. 303–4, but my translation; *HA*, pp. 359–60, lines 11958–65.
59. See Reinhard Buchwald: *Führer durch Goethes Faustdichtung* (Alfred Kröner Verlag, Stuttgart, 1955), p. 249.

forcibly reminds us of Faust's famous outburst to his disciple Wagner near the beginning of Part I: '*Zwei Seelen wohnen, ach! in meiner Brust,/Die eine will sich von der andern trennen . . .*' ('Two souls, alas! are housed within my breast,/And either would be parted from the other . . .').[60] The crux of his whole problematical career is pinpointed in these two lines and then abstractly generalized in the eight lines just quoted from Part II. Yet together (they each comment on the other) we are given an account both of Faustian nature and human nature in general which, in terms of warring or united opposites, is a mirror image of 'the Hermetic view that man had become divided within himself'.[61] Titus Burckhardt in his *Alchemy: Science of the Cosmos, Science of the Soul* illuminates this by contrasting the different procedure of mysticism:

> Speaking in general terms, mysticism's point of departure is that the soul has become alienated from God and turned towards the world. Consequently the soul must be reunited with God, and this it does by discovering in itself His immediate and all-illuminating presence. Alchemy, on the other hand, is based on the view that man, as a result of the loss of his original 'Adamic' state, is divided within himself. He regains his integral nature only when the two powers . . . are again reconciled with one another.[62]

The last two sentences here give a precise picture of Faust's state of soul in his *Zwei Seelen* speech as well as indirectly glossing 'The unified double-nature' mentioned by the More Perfect Angels, even if their purpose is one of purification; hence the separation of 'the elements' from the 'force of spirit' in Faust's present make-up, not their reconcilement. Nevertheless, with regard to this whole issue, it is of paramount importance that we keep in mind the following directive given by Albrecht Schöne in his commentary for Deutscher Klassiker's edition of *Faust*:

---

60. *HA*, p. 41, lines 1112–13; the first line here is Payne's translation (p. 67), the second my own.
61. Abraham, *A Dictionary of Alchemical Imagery*, p. 36.
62. Titus Burckhardt, *Alchemy: Science of the Cosmos, Science of the Soul* p. 149.

But rather than being a matter of crude, very un-Goethean dualism based on the 'separation' of spirit and matter, it is here a question of 'purification' appropriate to Goethe's theory of metamorphosis, which recalls alchemical processes—and a purification that separates and removes the 'turbid' quality of earthly impurities and entanglements of guilt from the 'pure' substance of the entelechy.[63]

This summarizes exactly the nature and upward path of Faust's post-mortem state as it progresses throughout the play's final scene, until we learn, just before the close from Gretchen, now *Una Poenitentium* (*One of the Penitents*), that '*Der früh Geliebte,/Nicht mehr Getrübte,/Er kommt zurück*' ('The early beloved,/No longer blemished,/He returns to me').[64] Faust's process of purification has now been completed: he is the *Nicht mehr Getrübte*—literally, 'He who is no longer turbid' or muddied, like unclear water. In his account just given, Albrecht Schöne has pinpointed the same German word in 'a purification that separates and removes the "*turbid*" quality of earthly impurities'. It is the penitent Gretchen, moreover, and no one else, not even the angels, who is able to effect this, since it is her love for Faust that lies behind the last two lines spoken by the More Perfect Angels quoted above: '*Die ewige Liebe nur/Vermag's zu scheiden*' ('Only eternal love is able/To separate these quite'), where the verb *scheiden* not only 'separates and removes' but is a chemical term meaning 'to refine'. Hence the alchemical is seen to hover behind the spiritual.

Now the essential Faustian drive, as understood by Goethe, is embodied in the theme or motif of striving (*Strebensmotiv*), which runs throughout the entire drama and marks out the hero's character, if not always his actions. So far, we have only touched on this, mainly in connection with its late modification in the great monologue which closes the opening scene of Part II. Basically, Goethe views this drive as something inherently positive, though fraught with dangers, since

63. Schöne, p. 802; my translation. Schöne can be seen to support Bortoft on Goethean science. cf. n. 32 above.
64. Norton, p. 307, but my translation; *HA*, p. 363, lines 12073–5.

it implies for him the striving after some kind of higher goal, however unspecified—a quest, if you like, for a nobler and finer condition of life. The Lord Himself in the *Prologue in Heaven* is clearly in support of all this when He tells Mephistopheles that '*Es irrt der Mensch, solang' er strebt*' ('Man will err as long as he strives'), at the same time countering this ten lines later with '*Ein guter Mensch in seinem dunklen Drange/Ist sich des rechten Weges wohl bewusst*' ('A good man in the darkness of his urges/Is still aware of which path is the right one').[65] And in the scene we have just been considering there is this summation, the last two lines of which have become famous:

> Gerettet ist das edle Glied
> Der Geisterwelt vom Bösen,
> Wer immer strebend sich bemüht,
> Den können wir erlösen.

> *This noble member of the spirit-world*
> *Is saved from evil:*
> *For he who endeavours to strive always,*
> *Him we can redeem.*[66]

Striving, therefore, can work both ways; and, as in Faust's own case, produces on the one hand tragic consequences, yet on the other a freeing from error in the long run. And there is a corollary that follows straight on:

> Und hat an ihm die Liebe gar
> Von oben teilgenommen,
> Begegnet ihm die selige Schar
> Mit herzlichem Willkommen.

---

65. *HA*, p. 18, lines 328–9; Payne, pp. 41–2, but my translation.
66. *HA*, p. 359, lines 11934–7; Norton, p. 303, but my translation.

And if love has taken part
In this from above,
Then the blessed troop will come
To meet him with heartfelt welcome.[67]

So that what we now get is a marriage of below with above, a movement upwards with a loving descent, in the form of a fusion of opposites, a *coniunctio oppositorum*. Transposing all this for a moment into Far-Eastern Buddhist terms, Faust's redemption at the end of Goethe's work is very much a combination, as it were, of Zen's self-struggle and self-striving with Pure Land or Amida Buddhism, where the believer places himself in the descending Buddha's hands as he is then welcomed into the Western Paradise. Not that I am suggesting that Goethe knew about these two ends of the Far-Eastern Buddhist spectrum, although more and more information on Buddhism and its traditions was beginning to infiltrate German professional and academic circles from the end of the eighteenth century onwards. However, a Western equivalent that he was very much aware of, and that features behind the scenes, so to speak, in his play's final episode, was the oppositional religious positions represented by Pelagianism and Augustinianism. In brief, the former, stemming from the British monk Pelagius (*c.* AD 354–418), stressed the primacy of human exertion in gaining spiritual salvation, likewise man's essential goodness, an orientation clearly embodied in Faust's striving; whereas the latter, deriving from Augustine of Hippo (AD 354–430), emphasized above all the centrality of divine grace in rescuing fallen man, an opposed orientation represented by Gretchen's love descending.

The movement onwards and/or upwards implicit in Faustian striving is, of course, fundamental to Faust's *Zwei Seelen* speech, where 'The one wishes to separate itself from the other'. Yet whereas

Die eine hält, in derber Liebeslust,
Sich an die Welt mit klammernden Organen;

---

67. HA, p. 359, lines 11938–41; Norton, p. 303, but my translation.

Die andre hebt gewaltsam sich vom Dust
Zu den Gefilden hoher Ahnen.

The one holds fast to the world in its crude passion
With all its clinging senses;
The other lifts itself up from the dust
Forcibly to the lofty fields of its ancestors.[68]

It is the latter soul here which encapsulates the striving side, the former embodying that sensuous attachment to things earthly which is characterized throughout the play by the so-called 'doctrine of the moment' and its accompanying 'pleasure principle' or enjoyment (*Genuss*), on which Faust's wager with Mephistopheles is based:

FAUST Werd' ich beruhigt je mich auf ein Faulbett legen,
So sei es gleich um mich getan!
Kannst du mich schmeichelnd je belügen,
Dass ich mir selbst gefallen mag,
Kannst du mich mit Genuss betrügen,
Das sei für mich der letzte Tag!
Die Wette biet' ich!
MEPHISTOPHELES   Topp!
FAUST   Und Schlag auf Schlag!
Werd' ich zum Augenblicke sagen:
Verweile doch! du bist so schön!
Dann magst du mich in Fesseln schlagen,
Dann will ich gern zugrunde gehn!

FAUST *If I be quieted with a bed of ease,*
Then let that moment be the end of me!
If ever flattering lies of yours can please
And soothe my soul to self-sufficiency,
And make me one of pleasure's devotees,

68. HA, p. 41, lines 1114–17; Payne, p. 67, but my translation.

> *Then take my soul, for I desire to die:*
> *And that's a wager!*

MEPHISTOPHELES   *Done!*

FAUST   *And done again!*
> *If to the fleeting hour I say*
> *'Remain, so fair thou art, remain!'*
> *Then bind me with your fatal chain,*
> *For I will perish in that day.*[69]

Of course Mephisto thinks he can provide Faust with a 'fleeting hour' or 'moment' (*Augenblick*) which will so appeal and seduce that he will easily win, since just before the wager he has said: 'I'll give you more/Than any mortal eye has seen before'; in connection with which he should have recalled Faust's comment on this: 'What, poor devil, have you to give?/Was ever a man's spirit in its lofty striving/By such as you understood?';[70] and indeed Mephisto's role and speeches throughout Goethe's play would seem to endorse that assessment. On the other hand, at a distance, as in the *Prologue in Heaven*, he astutely sees into his provisional victim's make-up with words that should have alerted him:

> Vom Himmel fordert er die schönsten Sterne
> Und von der Erde jede höchste Lust,
> Und alle Näh' und alle Ferne
> Befriedigt nicht die tiefbewegte Brust.

> *From Heaven he demands the loveliest stars*
> *And from the earth every intense delight,*
> *Yet all that is near and all that is far*
> *Cannot appease his deeply moved being.*[71]

---

69. *HA*, p. 57, lines 1692–1702; Payne, p. 87.
70. The German text in *HA*, p. 56, lines 1675–7; Payne, p. 86, but my translation.
71. *HA*, p. 27, lines 304–7; Payne, p. 41, but my translation.

This is in answer to the Lord's question as to whether he knows His servant Faust, a statement which then draws the admission from heaven's ruler that, although Faust at present '*nur verworren dient*' ('only serves confusedly'), He 'will soon be able to lead him into clarity', at which the Devil puts Him on the spot, as it were, by engaging Him in a wager as to who will win Faust's soul. Thus we have two wagers—the first between the Lord and the Devil, instituted by the latter, the second between Faust and the Devil, instituted by the former. In both cases Mephistopheles loses yet is instrumental to each. Indeed, the Lord makes it quite plain that, because of his tendency to rest on his laurels, man needs someone like the Devil to rouse him to activity (though Faust himself seems not at all to fit this category): '*Drum geb' ich gern ihm den Gesellen zu,/Der reizt und wirkt und muss als Teufel schaffen*'('Therefore I gladly permit him this companion,/ Who goads and activates and must create as devil').[72] This is not in the least so very far from Mephisto's own, admittedly sly, answer to Faust who asks him on entering: 'Who are you then?' and replies '*Ein Teil von jener Kraft,/Die stets das Böse will und stets das Gute schafft*' ('A part of that power/Which always desires evil and always creates good').[73] Significantly, in both quotes, the same verb 'create' (*schaffen*) is used. Thirteen lines later he extends his identity with '*Ich bin ein Teil des Teils, der anfangs alles war,/Ein Teil der Finsternis, die sich das Licht gebar*' ('Part of a part am I, that once was all,/A part of darkness, mother of the light'). From these three quotations it is clear that in Goethe's world good and evil are closely intertwined, not dualistically set apart and opposed, as with Taoism's *yin/yang* and the alchemical states of *nigredo* and *albedo*, with the latter emerging from the former as part of an ongoing (i.e. dissolving and coagulating) process of continuous transformation.

What this now brings us to is a central Goethean belief embodied in and throughout *Faust*, namely, the fundamental principle of *Polarität und Steigerung* ('polarity and intensification'), which we can

---

72. *HA*, p. 18, lines 342–3; Payne, p. 42, but my translation.
73. *HA*, p. 47, lines 1335–6; Payne, p. 75, but my translation.

best illustrate by the poet's late comment of 1828 on his youthful essay *Nature* written in 1783:

The realization, however, which is lacking (in that essay) is the perception of the two great driving-wheels of all nature: the concept of *polarity* and *intensification*. These belong to matter, in so far as we think materially; on the other hand to the spirit, in so far as we think spiritually. Matter exists in an endless state of attraction and repulsion, spirit is an ever-striving state of ascent. Since, however, matter never exists and is never effective without spirit, and spirit never without matter, thus matter is likewise able to become intensified just as the spirit insists on being attracted and repelled; in the same way as that person alone is capable of thinking who has sufficiently separated things out in order to link them up and link them up in order to be able to separate them out again.[74]

One notes the use of the phrase '*immerstrebendem Aufsteigen*' ('an ever-striving state of ascent') to categorize the spirit, '*immerwähren-dem Anziehen und Abstössen*' ('an endless state of attraction and repulsion') to categorize matter. At the same time both entities are said to possess the qualities of 'polarity and intensification'; hence are mutually cross-connected, as are the activities of the mind in thinking;[75] so that reality in all its manifestations is a visualized instance of what Henri Bortoft has termed 'the holistic mode of consciousness', as opposed to both Cartesian and analytic-empirical ways of thinking and perceiving.[76] Like Goethe, Jung also (as we shall

74. My translation; German text in HA 13, p. 48. Goethe's 1783 *Natur* essay can be found on pp. 45–7.

75. Cf. Jung, *Memories, Dreams, Reflections* (Fontana Library, 1972): 'Just as all energy proceeds from opposition, so the psyche too possesses its inner polarity, this being the indisputable pre-requisite for its aliveness, as Heraclitus realised long ago. Both theoretically and practically, polarity is inherent in all living things' (p. 379). Also Paul Roubiczek, *Thinking in Opposites* (1952).

76. See Bortoft, *The Wholeness of Nature*, pp. 53–4 and 99:

The error of empiricism rests on the fact that what it takes to be material objects see) endorsed life's polarities. So did Blake; as witness his famous pronouncement from the beginning of *The Marriage of Heaven and Hell* (1793):

Without Contraries is no progression. Attraction and Repulsion, Reason and Energy, Love and Hate, are necessary to Human existence. From these contraries spring what the religious call Good & Evil.[77]

Here 'Contraries' and 'progression' are the Blakean equivalent of 'polarity and intensification'. And like Blake, Goethe was certainly indebted to Jakob Boehme for the gist of this idea—with Heraclitus, whom Goethe had studied in Greek, in the background as far as polarity itself is concerned, as Jung has pointed out.[78] However, the poet's more dynamic concept of *Steigerung*, whereby the polar opposites intensify or heighten, then fuse or synthesize at a higher level, break

are condensations of meaning. When we see a chair, for example, we are seeing a condensed meaning and not simply a physical body. Since meanings are not objects of sensory perception, seeing a chair is not the sensory experience we imagine it to be. What empiricism, and common sense, miss through mistaking meaning for matter is the dimension of mind in cognitive perception. This is usually invisible to us because it is transparent in the act of cognitive perception, and hence we do not suspect that it is there. It is often only in cases where normal cognition is disrupted that the dimension of mind becomes visible.

What also hides this dimension from us is the presupposition that cognitive processes can be understood in the framework of the Cartesian divorce of subject from object, the separation of consciousness from world . . . . In other words, consciousness is always directed towards an object. Hence in cognitive perception there is an indissoluble unity between the conscious mind and the object of which it is conscious.

Further:

It was mentioned briefly in 'Modes of Consciousness' that a *relationship* cannot be experienced *as such* in the analytical mode of consciousness. Since in this mode it is the elements which are related that stand out in experience, the relationship itself can only seem to be a shadowy abstraction to the intellectual mind. The perception of a relationship *as such* would require a simultaneous perception of the whole, and hence the restructuring of consciousness into the holistic mode.

77. Blake: *Poems and Prophecies* (Everyman, 1991), introduction by Kathleen Raine, p. 43.

78. See n. 75 above.

apart, then again merge in what is a dialectical and, indeed, alchemical progression, undoubtedly stems from Renaissance Hermeticism, alchemy's philosophical wing, and also characterizes the triadic structure of Hegel's thought with its thesis, antithesis, and synthesis. To quote once more from M. H. Abrams's *Natural Supernaturalism* on this subject:

> The body of Hermetic literature is large, varied, and written in a fantastic symbolism which is designed to conceal its potent mysteries from the uninitiate; we are able, nevertheless, to make out a reiterative conceptual pattern . . . In this scheme there is a strong emphasis on polarity, conceived on the model of sexual opposites and regarded as the force that compels all natural processes. In addition, the overall course of things is envisioned as a circular movement from unity into multiplicity and, ultimately, back to unity.[79]

The idea of polarity here 'conceived on the model of sexual opposites' is totally alchemical, referring to the marriage of opposites, *coniunctio oppositorum*, marking the culmination of each of the four phases in the alchemical operation, where opposed substances and/or soul-forces unite and fuse in a sexual embrace of king with queen, Sol with Luna, brother with sister, sulphur with mercury, or cock with hen. Such coupling and melding images were continually represented in word and picture in a host of colourful and imaginative ways. And in *Faust* itself the ultimate *coniunctio* during its hero's earthly career, albeit in the form of what Goethe called 'A Classical-Romantic Phantasmagoria' which takes place partly in ancient Greece, partly in the Middle Ages, is exemplified by Helen of Troy's visit to Faust's medieval castle, where their wooing and union occur, resulting in the boy Euphorion who tragically, however, succumbs to an Icarus-type death in Arcadia.[80] Alice Raphael describes this final *coniunctio*, known in alchemy as 'the royal wedding', as follows:

79. Abrams, *Natural Supernaturalism*, p. 158.
80. See in Norton, pp. 231–55, the scene entitled *Inner Courtyard of a Castle*; HA, pp. 276–303, the latter half of which, unmarked as such in Norton, is headed *Schattiger Hain* (*Shady Grove*).

We are, therefore, justified in considering it (i.e. the Helena episode) to be a poetic representation of the *Mysterium Coniunctionis*, in which the King and the Queen[81]—analogous to Sol and Luna— bring to birth the Divine Child.

The *infans philosophorum* or 'philosophical child', as he or she was called, was synonymous with the philosophers' stone. The last sentence of the M. H. Abrams extract above, where he talks of 'the overall course of things' being envisaged as 'a circular movement from unity into multiplicity and, ultimately, back to unity', also corroborates the cyclic structure of *Faust* as an *opus circulatorium* that we noted earlier.[82]

However, it is crucial to emphasize that this structure does not simply mirror the circular emanationist thought of Neoplatonism, whatever its immensely fruitful contribution to and influence on both Renaissance and Romantic art and thinking, whereby we get a spiritual outflow radiating from the one cosmic source, then a reversion back to square one, as it were. Rather, as with *Faust* and as Abrams goes on to document with regard to Romanticism as a whole, we experience instead a fusion of 'the idea of the circular return with the idea of linear progress, to describe a distinctive figure of Romantic thought and imagination—the ascending circle, or spiral'.[83] This best scholar of English and German Romanticism then introduces the 'Romantic version of emanation and return' into his argument with direct relationship both to Goethe and Coleridge:

> According to this view, the reunion or synthesis which follows after any division into contraries constitutes a 'third thing' which is higher than the original unity because it preserves the distinction that it has overcome. Goethe's description of what he calls 'spiral' development uses the alchemical term *Steigerung* (enhancement)

81. Raphael, *Goethe and the Philosophers' Stone*, p. 188.
82. Cf. p. 55 above.
83. Abrams, *Natural Supernaturalism*, p. 184.

for this result: 'The two great drive-wheels of all nature' are 'the concept of polarity and of enhancement'. Every phenomenon must separate itself in order to manifest itself as a phenomenon, but 'the separate seeks itself again' and if 'the separate first enhances itself it brings forth through the union of the enhanced parts a third, new, higher, totally unexpected thing'. 'In Life, and in the view of a vital philosophy', as Coleridge put the concept, 'the two component counter-powers actually interpenetrate each other and generate a higher third, including both the former, 'ita tamen ut sit alia et major'.[84]

This is an excellent summation of the ruling ideas governing Goethe's drama, which enable us to highlight the fact that his alchemical concept of *Steigerung* (intensification/heightening/enhancement) is employed in conjunction with 'what he calls "spiral" development' or *Spiraltendenz*, a notion deriving from his theory of plant morphology and involving another key-concept—that of metamorphosis, as in the prose treatise, *Versuch die Metamorphose der Pflanzen zu erklären* (*Essay Explaining Plant Metamorphosis*) of 1790 and in verse-form with *Die Metamorphose der Pflanzen* of 1798. In a late essay entitled *Spiraltendenz der Vegetation* (*The Spiral Tendency of Vegetation*) (1831) we find this summary:

We have to take on board the following: that a universal tendency to form spirals governs the world of vegetation, by means of which,

84. Ibid. For the Coleridge quotation here, see the essay, 'The Statesman's Manual', Appendix C, p. 89, in *Collected Works* 6 (*Lay Sermons*) (Routledge, 1972); where the Latin phrase is translated as 'in such a way, however, that it is different and greater'. In a note to the passage just quoted, Abrams also makes two illuminating comparisons with contemporaries of Goethe: 'You are no chemist', Novalis remarked, 'or you would know that through genuine combination there ensues a third thing which is both at the same time, and more than both' (*Briefe und Werke*, III, 20). On Schiller's complex use of the concept of the 'third thing' which both mediates and preserves differentiation and contraries, see E. M. Wilkinson and L. Willoughby, (trans. and eds.), *Schiller's 'On the Aesthetic Education of Man'* (Oxford, 1967); e.g. pp. li–lii, xciii–xciv, 349–50 (pp. 505–6).

in conjunction with a vertical aspiration, the structure and forma-
tion of all plants are achieved according to the law of metamorphosis.[85]

With all this in mind, we can finally appreciate the import of Peter
Salm's *The Poem as Plant (A Biological View of Goethe's* Faust*)*,[86] in
which the author sees the play as a poetic organism, a kind of primal
plant or *Urpflanze* projected as a 'visible idea' creating structural and
thematic equivalents to plant metamorphosis: a *Polarität und Steigerung* that radiates a host of vegetative images and symbols. As a result,
the world of plant morphology would seem to join hands with the
world of alchemy, both being fundamentally organic not mechanical,
and equally geared to a realm of proliferating imaginative forms.

85. See *HA* 13, p. 135; my translation.
86. Published by Case Western Reserve University, 1971.

3

Arthur Schopenhauer and
the Thought of India

Stephen Cross

I<small>N</small> Chapter 1 we saw something of the effect which the discovery of Indian thought and literature late in the eighteenth century created in Germany, and in the present chapter we pick up these threads again as they appear in the thought of one of the great philosophers of the following century, Arthur Schopenhauer. It is interesting to note that as a young man Schopenhauer was for a short time in close contact with the subject of the previous chapter, Goethe. This was at Weimar during the early months of 1814, when Schopenhauer was twenty-five and Goethe already well past sixty.[1] Goethe's book *On the Theory of Colours* (*Zur Farbenlehre*) had appeared in 1810, but he was still actively working on his optical ideas and anti-Newtonian theory of colour. Interested by the ideas Schopenhauer had put forward in his earliest work, *On the Fourfold Root of the Principle of Sufficient Reason* (1813), Goethe showed the young and unknown philosopher his experiments and even lent him his apparatus so that he could repeat them for himself at home. A little after this Schopenhauer wrote a short work, calling it *On Vision and Colours* (*Über das Sehen und die Farben*) and sending it to Goethe in 1815;[2] however, the relationship, although close for a time, did not last—it was, Goethe wrote later, like the parting of friends who wish to go in different directions.[3]

---

1. Schopenhauer's mother, the novelist Johanna Schopenhauer, moved to Weimar in 1806, and in the years which followed Goethe was a frequent visitor to the literary *salon* at her house.

2. A Latin version of this work was published in 1816. The first chapter is printed as an Appendix to E. F. J. Payne's translation of *On the Fourfold Root of the Principle of Sufficient Reason* (Open Court, La Salle, Illinois, 1974).

3. Goethe wrote of his encounter with Schopenhauer: 'We dealt with many things in mutual agreement, but at last a certain division became inevitable, as when two

In spite of this early contact and his lasting admiration for Goethe—
'Goethe educated me anew,' he wrote later[4]—Schopenhauer's ideas
were developed independently and it was he who, perhaps more than
any other person, carried forward into the second half of the nineteenth century the ideas of the Oriental Renaissance and the enthusiasm for the thought of India which the discovery of Sanskrit
literature had generated. He related Indian philosophical ideas both
to his own thought and to that of Kant (and indeed of Plato), and in
this way a bridge was constructed by means of which Indian thought
started to become a part of the consciousness of educated Europeans.[5]
Thus one scholar writes that with Schopenhauer 'the stream of Indian
thought flows into the spirit of Europe with an unprecedented force
and depth';[6] another that 'no other Western philosopher so signalizes
the turn towards India as does Schopenhauer';[7] while the philosopher
himself writes in the Preface to his principal work, *The World as Will
and Representation* (*Die Welt als Wille und Vorstellung*) the following
significant words: 'If, I say, the reader has also already received and
assimilated the divine inspiration of Indian wisdom, then he is best of
all prepared to hear what I have to say to him. It will not speak to
him, as to many others, in a strange and even hostile tongue.'[8]

When, late in 1818, this book was published Schopenhauer was
aged thirty and the European discovery of Indian thought, although
still in its infancy, had passed through its initial phase. In the years
that followed he assiduously kept up with the new literature on India,

friends who have hitherto gone together say goodbye—the one, however, wanting to
go north, the other south, so that they very speedily lose sight of each other.' Cited in
Bryan Magee, *The Philosophy of Schopenhauer* (Clarendon Press, Oxford, 1997), p. 17.

4. Cited in Magee, *Philosophy of Schopenhauer*, p. 16.

5. Paul Deussen, equally learned in Indian thought and the philosophy of Schopenhauer—he was called by Nietzsche 'Schopenhauer's most devoted admirer'—played
a leading part in this development.

6. Franz Mockrauer, 'Schopenhauer und Indien', in *Jahrbuch der Schopenhauer-
Gesellschaft* 15 (1928), p. 6.

7. W. Halbfass, *Indian and Europe: An Essay in Philosophical Understanding* (Moti-
lal Banarsidass, Delhi, 1990), p. 105.

8. A. Schopenhauer, *The World as Will and Representation*, trans. E. F. J. Payne
(Dover Publications, New York, 1966), hereafter *WWR*, vol. 1, p. xv.

becoming one of the earliest Europeans to acquire a good knowledge of Hindu and Buddhist philosophical and religious ideas. At the time of his death in 1860 his library contained almost as much on India and the East as on the classical civilizations of Greece and Rome, something very unusual for the time, and even now he is the only major European philosopher who has consistently given importance to Eastern thought. Bryan Magee, in his excellent study of Schopenhauer's ideas, has written that he 'remains the only great Western philosopher to have been genuinely well versed in Eastern thought, and to have related it to his own work'.[9]

The relation of Schopenhauer's thought to that of India is best considered under two aspects. First, there is the parallel between his epistemology—that side of his thought which examines the basis of our knowledge of the world and which he called (to borrow from the title of his book) *the world as Representation*—and the Indian concept of *Maya*, or *illusion* as this term is often loosely translated. This parallel is something which has long been known, and indeed it was Schopenhauer himself who first pointed it out. The second way in which his thought is close to that of India is much less well known. It concerns the other main aspect of his philosophy, that is to say his ontology or what he termed *the world as Will*. This, as we shall see subsequently, offers striking similarities to the Indian concept of *shakti* or 'power'; and in this case the parallel is the more remarkable for the fact that in Schopenhauer's time the concept of *shakti* was hardly known to Europeans.

This is not the place to enter into Schopenhauer's life in any detail and we will do no more than briefly fill in the background. He was born in 1788 and died at Frankfurt in 1860. He came from an old and wealthy merchant family, a sort of commercial aristocracy long associated with the Hanseatic city of Danzig on the Baltic. He had to struggle hard to escape from a lifetime in the family business, and consequently got to university much later than most young men. Yet by the time he was thirty he had formulated his philosophy and

9. Magee, *Philosophy of Schopenhauer*, p. 15.

written his most significant book, the first volume of *The World as Will and Representation*. The second volume of this work was published much later, in 1844: it adds a great deal of very interesting further evidence and argumentation, but does not alter the thesis contained in the first volume.

When it was initially presented to the public in 1818 *The World as Will and Representation* was for Schopenhauer a disaster. Hardly anyone reviewed it, and most of the copies were sold off as waste paper. Perhaps Schopenhauer, who had a prickly character which he learned to tame only after many years, was in part to blame. As a young man he came into contact with some of the leading figures of the day in Germany, among them Fichte, Hegel, Ludwig Tieck and Goethe, but of all these it was only with Goethe that he was able to establish a good relationship and this, as we have seen, lasted only briefly. Goethe hardly speaks of the philosopher after their parting, and seems to have done nothing to help his book when it was published five years later.

Schopenhauer did not marry and was fortunate in having sufficient private means to live on. After the publication of his principal work had failed he lived alone in Frankfurt studying and writing systematically on his own, which cannot have been easy in face of the neglect he experienced. Only in the final decade of his life did he start to receive recognition, and this first came from an English critic, John Oxenford, whose long and perceptive essay on Schopenhauer's writings appeared in *The Westminster Review* in 1853 and was quickly reprinted in Germany.[10] Subsequently Wagner and Nietzsche were among Schopenhauer's earliest and most enthusiastic disciples, although neither of them met with him.

After his death his fame grew rapidly as he had forseen, and he became the most widely read and discussed philosopher of the second half of the nineteenth century. The list of significant figures, particularly among creative writers, who came under his influence is a

10. J. Oxenford, 'Iconoclasm in German Philosophy', in *The Westminster Review*, vol. 59, pp. 388–407. Bryan Magee points out that the periodical was at this time being edited by George Eliot, who must therefore have been one of the first in England to become aware of Schopenhauer.

remarkable one.[11] Nevertheless, a reaction set in and for much of the twentieth century Schopenhauer was decidedly out of fashion.[12] In the English-speaking world especially his reputation was eclipsed by that of Nietzsche who, in spite of eventually repudiating Schopenhauer's ideas and in some respects reversing his system, owed a great deal to him. In recent decades the situation has changed again, and there is once more growing interest in Schopenhauer.

As we saw in Chapter 1, the thinkers of the Romantic movement were a powerful force in Germany during the years when Schopenhauer was growing to maturity. In some ways he was of their number, in others decidedly not. We find impassioned descriptions in his youth of the mountains he ascended in the high Alps, very much in the style of the romantic young men depicted in the paintings of Caspar David Friedrich.[13] The way in which the arts were understood in the new Romantic literature affected him and remains apparent in his later writing; music, especially, he loved, writing of 'that profound pleasure with which we see the deepest recesses of our nature find expression'.[14] And, again like the Romantics, he was strongly drawn to the European mystics: he greatly admired, for example, the French seventeenth-century writer, Madame Guyon, 'that great and beautiful soul, whose remembrance always fills me with reverence'.[15]

On the other hand, Schopenhauer appreciated clarity of thought

11. In addition to Wagner and Nietzsche, the following were, at various times, significantly influenced by Schopenhauer's thought: Tolstoy, Turgenev, Maupassant, Zola, Proust, Strindberg, Mahler, D'Annunzio, Pirandello, Conrad, Thomas Hardy, D. H. Lawrence, Thomas Mann, and Wittgenstein.

12. Bertrand Russell, in the short chapter on Schopenhauer in his *History of Western Philosophy* (1946), seems more interested in emphasizing the philosopher's personal failings than in exploring his ideas. And Bryan Magee (*Philosophy of Schopenhauer*, p. 96) writes of 'the distinguished people who taught me philosophy at Oxford in the 1950s' that 'scarcely any of them had read Schopenhauer'.

13. On Schopenhauer's youthful excursions into the mountains see R. Safranski, *Schopenhauer and the Wild Years of Philosophy* (Harvard University Press, 1990), pp. 50–51.

14. *WWR*, vol. 1, p. 256. For Schopenhauer's very interesting discussion of the nature of music (which Wagner subsequently endorsed) see pp. 256–67.

15. *WWR*, vol. 1, p. 385.

and was unimpressed by most of the leading exponents of the Romantic movement. Nor do we find him reacting against the Enlightenment in the manner of the German Romantics. His thought in some respects is closer to English attitudes. He spoke almost perfect English— the result of a miserable six months at a boarding school in Wimbledon!—and like the English, his arguments are often based on careful observation of the world and human behaviour, with the result that he can be quite empirical and down-to-earth.[16] Concepts, he tells us time and again, are only of value in so far as they rest upon a firm foundation of empirical reality; on 'real life and its hurly-burly', as he puts it.[17] Then, indeed, they are powerful instruments enabling us to examine and explore the meaning of both outer and inner experience. But concepts that cannot be traced back to experience are like notes issued by a bank which has nothing to back them with: they 'move in the air without support', floating off into a cloud-cuckoo land that simply does not exist. This, Schopenhauer thought, is what had happened in the case of Hegel.[18]

In these ways, then, Schopenhauer was well removed from the Romantics, but there was certainly one respect in which he was close to them. This was the idea, going back to the Florentine Renaissance, that there is a single core of truth linking together the major religions of the past (and much of the philosophy also); a truth which has become obscured and lost, but which perhaps still lies hidden in some far off land and is capable of recovery. We saw in Chapter 1 the importance this idea had for writers like Schelling, Novalis and Friedrich Schlegel, and Schopenhauer equals them in his commitment to it. The notion of a rediscovery, and perhaps indeed a perfecting, of ancient wisdom is undoubtedly present in his writings and has much to do with the interest Indian thought held for him.

Schopenhauer first came into significant contact with Indian

16. See p. xxiii of the Foreword by Richard Taylor in E. von der Luft, *Schopenhauer: New Essays in Honor of his 200th Birthday* (Edwin Mellen Press, Lampeter, 1988).

17. A. Schopenhauer, *On the Basis of Morality*, trans. E. F. J. Payne (Berghahn Books, Providence and Oxford, 1995), p. 120.

18. *WWR*, vol. 1, p. 273.

thought while staying at Weimar and moving in the circle of Goethe. Here, at the end of 1813, he met the orientalist Friedrich Majer, who introduced the young philosopher to a book which was to be of the utmost importance to him for the rest of his life. This was the *Oupnek'hat*, a title which, as we saw in Chapter 1, is a Persian form of the Sanskrit word *Upanishad*. It was by any standard an extraordinary publication. The Upanishads, up until then unknown to Europe, stand at the very heart of Hindu thought, and the *Oupnek'hat* contained not just the twelve or thirteen principal texts which is what we usually mean today when we speak of the Upanishads, but many of the lesser and later ones as well, a total of fifty in all. These had been assembled in the middle of the seventeenth century by Indian scholars and then translated into the literary language of the Mughal Empire, Persian. The whole project was carried out on the personal initiative of one man, Prince Dara Shukoh,[19] the eldest son and heir-apparent of the Mughal Emperor of India, Shah Jahan—ruler of one of the most splendid empires in the world and builder of the Taj Mahal.

Prince Dara Shukoh was a Sufi and believed strongly in the underlying unity of the great religious traditions of the world. He was especially interested in parallels between the spiritual path of the Sufis and that of Hindu mystics, and for this reason wanted to make the Upanishads available in Persian. Not long after the translation was completed Prince Dara was overthrown by his younger brother Aurangzeb, who seized the Mughal throne in a brief but bloody war of succession; Dara's interest in the Upanishads and Hindu mysticism was used to justify this seizure of power and he was executed on the grounds of apostasy from Islam. More than a century later a copy of this Persian text of the Upanishads came into the hands of the French scholar Anquetil Duperron, who translated it from Persian into Latin; and in this way, the Upanishads became available for the first time to Europe. This Latin version was the book which came into the young Schopenhauer's hands as *The Oupnek'hat*.

19. On Dara Shukoh and the translation of the Upanishads see S. Cross, 'Ex Oriente Lux: How the Upanishads Came to Europe', in *Temenos Academy Review* 2 (spring 1999), pp. 106–29.

In spite of being a double-translation and at first sight a discon-
certing medley of Persian and Latin terms, the *Oupnek'hat* had considerable merits which Schopenhauer was quick to perceive. First of
all, it was the most comprehensive collection of the Upanishads, hence
of the philosophical literature associated with Hinduism, to appear in
the West right up to the time of Paul Deussen's translation of *Sixty
Upanishads* late in the nineteenth century.[20] Second, both translations—Dara Shukoh's from Sanskrit into Persian and Duperron's
from the Persian into Latin—had been undertaken with exceptional
care and an acute sense of the significance of the original texts. And
third, the Upanishads it contains are embedded in an extensive explanatory commentary (which has, however, the disadvantage that it is
not clearly distinguished from the text itself), which is based on
Shankara's celebrated interpretation and greatly illuminates the often
obscure text. In addition to this, Duperron himself added what amounts
to a second layer of commentary in the form of extensive notes. Thus
the whole, while not without its faults,[21] amounts to a very substantial
body of work—by far the most extensive presentation of ancient
Indian philosophical and religious ideas available to Europe in the
first half of the nineteenth century.

While it was not Schopenhauer's only source for Hindu thought,
the *Oupnek'hat* was of the highest importance to him and he speaks
of it as 'the greatest gift to the nineteenth century'.[22] He studied it
carefully and repeatedly throughout the remainder of his life—more
than forty-five years—writing in the last of his published works:

How thoroughly redolent of the holy spirit of the Vedas is the *Oup-
nekhat*! How deeply stirred is he who, by diligent and careful

---

20. Paul Deussen, *Sechzig Upanishad's des Veda*, 1897.

21. The orientalist Max Müller wrote of the *Oupnek'hat* that it was 'written in so
utterly unintelligible a style, that it required the lynxlike perspicacity of an intrepid
philosopher, such as Schopenhauer, to discover a thread through such a labyrinth'.
Sacred Books of the East, vol. 1: *The Upanishads* (Clarendon Press, Oxford, 1879),
pp. lviii–lix.

22. *WWR*, vol. 1, p. 355.

reading, is now conversant with the Persian-Latin rendering of this incomparable book! How imbued is every line with firm, definite, and harmonious significance! On every page we come across profound, original, and sublime thoughts, whilst a lofty and sacred earnestness pervades the whole. Here everything breathes the air of India and radiates an existence that is original and akin to nature ... With the exception of the original text, it is the most profitable and sublime reading that is possible in the world; it has been the consolation of my life and will be that of my death.[23]

Let us now turn aside to glance briefly at Schopenhauer's relationship with the other great religion of India, Buddhism. To see this in its proper context of the thought of the Romantic era in Europe, we cannot do better than begin with the words of the distinguished scholar of Buddhism, Edward Conze, who writes:

In the aftermath of the French revolution, many of the basic laws of the spiritual life were re-discovered by great poets who were also fine thinkers, such as Blake, Shelley, Wordsworth, and Coleridge in England. Though often vitiated by a fatal rift between theory and practice, their thought offers many parallels to Buddhist thinking. To this generation of rebels against the Goddess of Reason belonged Arthur Schopenhauer, whose thought, partly under Indian influence, exhibits numerous, and almost miraculous, coincidences with the basic tenets of Buddhist philosophy.[24]

Schopenhauer's thought is indeed close to Buddhism in important respects, and this is the more remarkable since it was not until he was approaching the age of forty that he was able to obtain a reasonably accurate knowledge of this religion. For a surprisingly long time the concept of Buddhism as a single religion was hardly understood in

---

23. A. Schopenhauer, *Parerga and Paralipomena*, trans. E. F. J. Payne (Clarendon Press, Oxford, 1974), vol. 2, p. 397.

24. Edward Conze: *Thirty Years of Buddhist Studies* (Cassirer, Oxford, 1967), p. 222.

the West; the various names under which the Buddha went in different parts of Asia—Shakyamuni, Fo, etc.—and the widely different cults to be found in China, Burma, Tibet, Japan, Mongolia, Thailand and other lands confusing the issue and preventing a clear understanding of the unity of the religion and its Indian source. But when, from about 1825 onwards, better information started to appear Schopenhauer seized upon it at once. He was among the first in Europe to grasp clearly that Buddhism is a single religion which, originating in India, had spread from there in varied forms across the whole of Asia. For the rest of his life he kept himself accurately informed, studying almost everything of importance published on Buddhism in German, French or English.

And of course he was much interested to discover that in some respects Buddhism was even closer to his own doctrines than were the Hindu teachings he had found in the Upanishads.[25] In later life, in spite of having no means of practising the religion, he sometimes referred to himself as a Buddhist; and his most prized possession, apart from the *Oupnek'hat*, was a rare image of the Buddha which he had been able to obtain from Paris. A visitor to his apartment towards the end of his life, Karl Bähr, recorded the following incident:

'Since we are talking about revelation', said Schopenhauer, 'I should show you something extremely rare and interesting.' With these words he brought a small sitting figure, not taller than one foot, from a corner of the room. This blackened iron or brass figure somehow resembled at first glance a Chinese pagoda. He put it in front of us on a table, while asking mysteriously if I could guess what it represented? I supposed it to be something Chinese; but he said that it probably originated from Tibet, was presumably hundreds of years old, and represented the Buddha. He emphasised that this was a rare and precious sculpture which he had obtained from Paris, and which I scarcely would encounter anywhere else. This

25. In a letter of 27 February 1856, to A. L. von Doss, Schopenhauer writes, 'Altogether the agreement with my doctrine is wonderful.'

statue, he explained, is as significant to Buddhists as is a cruxifix to Christians; the Buddha is depicted here as a beggar. When I asked him why Buddha was portrayed here as a beggar he began to tell me the Buddha legend, but in such a way that I have never been able to forget it. This was not an armchair scholar, not a dry German academic, a dry philosophy professor, but a philosopher by the grace of God, a sage of antiquity who spoke to me. I had to listen to him with awe and devotion.[26]

A little after this Schopenhauer had this statue carefully gilded, and it occupied a place of honour in his apartment. There were three features of Buddhist teaching which particularly attracted his attention. First, the fact that Buddhism admits no Creator-God (the latter being, in Schopenhauer's opinion, a Jewish invention). Second, the exalted nature of Buddhism's moral code, its strong emphasis on compassion and the manner in which this is extended to animals. And third, the teaching that *nirvana* entails a complete surrender of individuality, and that in consequence its positive nature lies outside all possibility of description, since descriptions can apply only to the individual nature and its experiences. Schopenhauer also observed that Buddhism is more directly philosophical and less prone to presentation in the form of myth than other religions; the Buddha, he thought, taught the pure doctrine free of mythological disguise. In 1844 he summed up his attitude in these words:

If I wished to take the results of my philosophy as the standard of truth, I should have to concede to Buddhism pre-eminence over the others. In any case, it must be a pleasure to me to see my doctrine in such close agreement with a religion that the majority of men on earth hold as their own ... And this agreement must be yet the more pleasing to me, inasmuch as in my philosophizing I have certainly not been under its influence. For up till 1818, when

26. Cited in D. W. Dauer, *Schopenhauer as Transmitter of Buddhist Ideas* (Herbert Lang, Berne, 1969), pp. 5–6.

my work appeared, there were to be found in Europe only a very few accounts of Buddhism, and those extremely incomplete and inadequate.[27]

Having briefly sketched our philosopher's relationship to Indian thought it is time to turn to his own ideas. Let us begin with what he called *the world as Representation*. What does he mean by this expression? The German word translated as *representation* is *Vorstellung*, and it signifies something which is 'placed before' one, not as an external sensuous object but as an internal idea, a mental picture. What Schopenhauer wishes to convey by his use of the word is the fact that the world we experience exists for each of us as a mental picture which arises in or is *placed before* our consciousness.[28] All that each one of us actually knows or experiences is what appears in our consciousness; and whether the images in consciousness correspond to something which exists outside, independent of our consciousness, is what philosophy must investigate.[29] In volume 2 of *The World as Will and Representation*, published in 1844, Schopenhauer writes these significant words (emphasis in the original):

For only after men had tried their hand for thousands of years at merely *objective* philosophizing did they discover that, among the many things that make the world so puzzling and precarious, the first and foremost is that, however immeasurable and massive it may be, its existence hangs nevertheless on a single thread; and this thread is the actual consciousness in which it exists. This condition, with which the existence of the world is irrevocably encumbered, marks it with the stamp of *ideality*, in spite of all *empirical* reality, and consequently with the stamp of the mere *phenomenon*.[30]

Schopenhauer places much emphasis on the fact that perception, as opposed to sensation (i.e. the changes experienced by the body), is

27. WWR, vol. 2, p. 169.   28. WWR, vol. 1, p. 3.   29. WWR, vol. 1, p. 3.
30. WWR, vol. 2, pp. 3–4.

intellectual, and that in consequence experience and the world which is experienced are also intellectual in origin.[31] Here, of course, he draws upon the conclusions which Kant had reached several decades earlier in *The Critique of Pure Reason*. Kant, he believed, was the greatest thinker the West had produced since the collapse of the ancient world,[32] and this was because he had succeeded in demonstrating incontrovertibly that this world which stands before us in consciousness is subjectively conditioned. That is to say, it is dependent upon the inherent and inborn structure of our minds; on what Schopenhauer calls 'an exceedingly complicated physiological process in the brain of an animal, the result of which is the consciousness of a *picture* there'.[33] It is these pictures in the mind which form the world that we experience—the world as Representation. In the continuation of the passage cited above, he affirms:

Thus the world must be recognized, from one aspect at least, as akin to a dream, indeed as capable of being put in the same class with a dream. For the same brain-function that conjures up during sleep a perfectly objective, perceptible, and indeed palpable world must have just as large a share in the presentation of the objective world of wakefulness. Though different as regards their matter, the two worlds are nevertheless obviously moulded from one form. This form is the intellect, the brain-function.[34]

Schopenhauer was in agreement with Kant as well as with the Romantic thinkers in holding that the human mind is not a *tabula rasa*, not simply a passive recipient of sense impressions. It plays an active role in shaping and organizing the material supplied by the senses. In particular, our ideas of time and space do not, as earlier

---

31. *WWR*, vol. 1, p. 12.

32. *WWR*, vol. 1, p. 425. See also p. 416, where Schopenhauer refers to the 'new and great knowledge' which Kant had brought, and *Parerga and Paralipomena*, vol. 1, p. 170, where he writes: 'For Kant has perhaps the most original mind ever produced by nature.'

33. *WWR*, vol. 1, p. ix.   34. *WWR*, vol. 2, p. 4.

thinkers had assumed, come to us from outside and as the result of observation. They are, on the contrary, inborn, part of the mind, the way it is structured, the way it operates. To use Kant's term, time and space are the *pure forms of intuition* by which our sense impressions are given form and organized into a meaningful pattern. Schopenhauer therefore called time and space the *principium individuationis,* since it is they which form the basis upon which the world of individual existences arises.[35]

Equally important for him is the fact that the idea of cause and effect is likewise inherent in the mind. Causality is not something we deduce from observation, as had been supposed, but something we already know, knowledge we are already born with.[36] Like our knowledge of time and space, it is inherent in the mind. We simply know, every child and every animal knows, that each physical event will bring with it a result, that one thing causes another. This knowledge is inborn, and without it no animal could survive for it provides the means by which we link together and interpret sense impressions and relate them to ourselves.

In this way Kant, as Schopenhauer puts it, '[took] to pieces the whole machinery of our cognitive faculty, by means of which the phantasmagoria of the objective world is brought about'.[37] He showed that time, space and causality are not drawn from experience, but pre-exist in the mind; they are known to us, in Kant's words, 'prior to all actual perception', or *a priori*,[38] and together make possible the appearance in consciousness of the empirical world. They are, Schopenhauer tells us, using the language of Kant, *transcendental* in nature;

35. Schopenhauer writes in *On the Basis of Morality,* (trans. E. F. J. Payne, Berghahn Books, Providence and Oxford, 1995), p. 206: 'Since homogeneous plurality consists of *individuals,* I call space and time, on the strength of their making plurality possible, the *principium individuationis,* and am not concerned whether this is precisely the sense in which the schoolmen took the expression.' See also WWR, vol. 1, pp. 352 and 378, where Schopenhauer equates the *principium individuationis* with the veil of Maya known to Indian thought.

36. WWR, vol. 1, p. 13.   37. WWR, vol. 1, p. 420.

38. Kant, *Critique of Pure Reason,* trans. N. Kemp Smith (Macmillan, London, 1950), p. 82.

that is, they are *prior to* or *transcend* the empirical world. They constitute the formal element in our knowledge, existing quite independently of experience and not derived from it.[39] They are part and parcel of the mind's structure, and therefore belong to the subject and not to the external world. Kant writes: 'if the subject . . . be removed, the whole constitution and all the relations of objects in space and time, nay space and time themselves, would vanish. As appearances, they cannot exist in themselves, but only in us'.[40] In accordance with this, Schopenhauer argues that space, time and causality are laws not of the existence of things, but rather the laws of our *representation* of things.[41] They are, as he puts it in a characteristically blunt turn of phrase, 'in man's head'—internally existing mental structures, and not, as previously assumed, external realities having an objective and absolute validity.[42] 'Before Kant,' he writes, 'it may be said, we were in time; now time is in us.'[43]

In this very different conception of the nature of the world we see emerging once more that strong tendency to privilege the inward nature and the mind which is characteristic of German thought as a whole. It is precisely the reassertion of the priority of the inner nature of man, after its temporary eclipse under the combined influence of French rationalism and British empiricism, which is expressed in the *Sturm und Drang* and by the Romantic movement as a whole, and also, in a very different form, in Kant's *Critique of Pure Reason*. The dominance of the subject over the external world of objects was for the early Romantic thinkers the all-important point of Kant's thinking, the central source of their inspiration. And here Schopenhauer is at one with them. Recalling, perhaps, his work with Goethe on the theory of colours, he writes, 'Just as our eye produces green, red, and blue, so does *our brain* produce, *time, space,* and *causality* (whose objectified abstraction is *matter*).'[44] Matter, he argues, is nothing but the creation of our inborn notion of causality. It is something which

39. *Parerga and Paralipomena*, vol. 1, p. 82.
40. *Critique of Pure Reason*, p. 82. See also p. 354 for a similar passage.
41. WWR, vol. 1, p. 426.   42. WWR, vol. 1, p. 420–21.
43. *Parerga and Paralipomena*, vol. 1, p. 85.   44. Ibid., p. 86, footnote.

we project as a cause to explain the various sensations which come to us. It is not a substance existing independently of mental perception, but an appearance. It exists in the mind of the perceiving subject and is not truly an external reality, although it appears as such.[45] And so, in a striking formulation, he tells us that, 'Materialism is the philosophy of the subject who forgets to take account of himself.'[46]

For Schopenhauer, then, it is upon our inborn ideas of space, time and causality that the whole of our experience of the world rests, and it is by means of them and the laws belonging to them that the entire universe takes on shape and form in our consciousness. Thus what we see and feel and know in outer experience is appearance and not true reality. Kant had established a distinction between what he termed *phenomena*—the perceptions arising in our mind—and *noumena*, or things as they are in themselves, that is to say, whatever it is which stands behind the pictures which arise in our mind. What this reality, these *things-in-themselves* are, Kant was unable to say, but he was certain that there must be such realities. In this way, Schopenhauer tells us, Kant made clear the great separation of our inherent or *a priori* knowledge from our *a posteriori* or normal, empirical knowledge derived from the world: and he did this with such clarity and precision that the distinction between the phenomenon and the thing-in-itself lying hidden behind it obtained an infinitely greater significance and a very much deeper meaning than before.[47]

Thus for both Kant and Schopenhauer the world of phenomena, the world we know and live in, exists as a creation in the minds of living beings. Here it is real enough, and in the collective consciousness which we all share it can certainly be said to exist. But it is not absolutely real; it has no objective reality outside that consciousness. It is the shadow-world which the prisoners in Plato's Myth of the Cave perceive—and indeed it is this doctrine of the illusory nature of the world which, in Schopenhauer's view, lies at the very heart of Plato's thought.[48] This, then, in brief outline, is the meaning of the

45. *WWR*, vol. 1, pp. 8–11.   46. *WWR*, vol. 2, p. 13.
47. *WWR*, vol. 1, pp. 418–19.   48. *WWR*, vol. 1, p. 419.

first aspect of Schopenhauer's philosophy, what he calls the world as *Representation*. Here is his own summary as we find it in his book *On the Basis of Morality*:

> If in the information that is given to the world by the marvellous depth of Kant's mind there is *anything* that is true beyond all doubt, it is the *Transcendental Aesthetic*, the doctrine of the ideality of space and time . . . It is Kant's triumph, one of the extremely few metaphysical doctrines that can be regarded as actually proved and as real conquests in the field of metaphysics. According to it, space and time are the forms of our own faculty of intuitive perception; they belong to this, and not to the things that are known through it. They can therefore never be a disposition of things-in-themselves but belong only to the *phenomenal appearance* of them, such as is only possible in our consciousness of the external world, which is tied to physiological conditions. But if *time* and *space* are foreign to the thing-in-itself, to the true essence of the world, so too must *plurality* be. Consequently, that which shows itself in the countless phenomena of this world of the senses can only be one thing; and only the one and identical essence can manifest itself in all those phenomena. And conversely, what exhibits itself as a *plurality* and consequently in time and space, cannot be a thing-in-itself, but only a *phenomenal appearance*. As such, however, this exists merely for our consciousness, which is limited by many different conditions and in fact depends on an organic function. Outside this consciousness, the phenomenon does not exist.[49]

What especially interested Schopenhauer was the fact that this teaching, that all plurality is only apparent and that behind it there stands a reality of another order, was not new. Although only recently arrived at by European philosophy, it was, he considered, the rediscovery of a great truth which had been known long before. It is, as we have seen, to be found in Plato, and is still more clearly evident in the

49. *On the Basis of Morality*, pp. 206–7.

ancient thought of India. Here it takes the form of the doctrine of Two Truths (*satya-dvaya*), a teaching present in the *Oupnek'hat* and also important for Buddhism, in which a clear distinction is made between the 'relative truth' (*samvriti-satya*), i.e., the truth of the empirical world and of individual being, and the 'highest' or absolute truth (*paramartha-satya*). The relative or lower truth is the knowledge of the world experienced by everyone prior to enlightenment, and consists of a network of relativities; it is the empirical world of subject-object relations, of names and things named.

Quite different from this is the 'highest truth'. This is truth itself, truth absolute; knowledge of the real as it is, without any distortion and beyond the intervention of the mind. It is beyond all categories of thought and every point of view. It knows the real directly, is entirely free from conceptual construction and beyond the scope of discursive thought, language and empirical activity.[50] Nagarjuna, the great Mahayana teacher who lived not long after the time of Christ, sums all this up as follows:

The teaching of the Dharma by the various Buddhas is based on the two truths; namely the relative (or worldly) truth and the absolute (or supreme) truth. Those who do not know the distinction between the two truths cannot understand the profound nature of the Buddha's teaching.[51]

In the Hindu tradition the same doctrine of Two Truths is stated by the greatest interpreter of the Upanishads, Shankara, in the following words:

The entire complex of phenomenal existence is considered as true as long as the knowledge of Brahman being the Self of all has not arisen; just as the phantoms of a dream are considered to be true

50. On the Buddhist teaching of Two Truths see T. R. V. Murti, *The Central Philosophy of Buddhism* (Allen and Unwin, London, 1960), pp. 207ff. and 244ff.

51. Nagarjuna, *Mulamadhyamaka-karika* 24.8–9, trans. K. Inada (Hokuseido Press, Tokyo, 1970).

until the sleeper wakes . . . The case is analogous to that of a dreaming man who in his dream sees manifold things, and, up to the moment of waking, is convinced that his ideas are produced by real perception without suspecting the perception to be a merely apparent one.[52]

Here we see the idea of *Maya*, illusion or appearance, which is deeply rooted in Indian thought—the idea that the world we live in is analogous to a collective dream having only a temporary and provisional reality, and that beyond it there lies another order of being, Brahman or absolute Reality, which we have access to only when, seeing through the veil of *Maya*, we attain liberation.

Throughout his life Schopenhauer drew strength from the belief that the concept of the world as *representation* which he had formulated was essentially at one both with the thought of Plato and with that of ancient India. He often draws attention to this in his writings,[53] and to him it meant that his doctrines were unlikely to be merely his own subjective inventions, but belonged to the perennial tradition of human wisdom. It meant that after centuries of wandering in the dark, European philosophy had rediscovered the same fundamental insights which had been perceived by the greatest minds of the past. Kant, however, had presented this doctrine, not in terms of poetic myth as Plato had done, but with a new and startling clarity, 'in an entirely new and original way', making it 'a proved and incontestable truth through the most calm and dispassionate presentation'. Schopenhauer adds that 'such clear knowledge and calm, deliberate presentation of this dreamlike quality of the whole world is really the basis of the whole Kantian philosophy; it is its soul and its greatest merit'.[54]

Nevertheless, there remains something which is unexplained: even though it is our mind with its inbuilt structure of time, space and

---

52. Shankara: *Commentary on the Vedanta-sutras* 2.1.14, trans. G. Thibaut, vol.1, p. 324 (Sacred Books of the East, vol. 34, Oxford University Press, Oxford, 1904).

53. See for example WWR, vol. 1, p. xv (Preface); also pp. 7–8.

54. WWR, vol. 1, pp. 419–20.

causality which presents to consciousness the empirical world and its phenomena, it is sense-impressions which trigger the mind's activity. But what gives rise to these sense-impressions? In what, if any, reality lying *outside* the mind and existing independently from it are they grounded? Or, putting the question a little differently, what is the factor—the *noumenon*, as Kant termed it—which gives to the world of empirical experience its apparently objective nature? Kant was certain there must be such a factor and called it the *thing-in-itself*; but this phrase is no more than a convenient label and does nothing to tell us what its nature is. Schopenhauer expresses this in the shape of a simple formula: 'My intuitive perception of a body in space is the product of my sense-function and brain-function with X.'[55] As is well known, Kant had concluded that this X, the thing-in-itself, cannot be known, since the mind cannot penetrate beyond the representations which it generates and which form the medium of its activity. Schopenhauer's solution brings us to the second aspect of his philosophy, to what he called the world as *Will*.

Up until now, of course, Schopenhauer has been treading in the footsteps of Kant, but the concept of the world as *Will* was a leap of the imagination which broke through the impasse represented by the unknowable character of Kant's thing-in-itself. It will be remembered that in the passage quoted a little earlier from *On the Basis of Morality* Schopenhauer argues that, since plurality is a creation of the mind, the true essence of the world, that which shows itself in the countless phenomena, 'can only be one thing; and only the one and identical essence can manifest itself in all those phenomena'. Thus in place of Kant's multiple things-in-themselves, Schopenhauer posits a single metaphysical existence, which might indeed take on multifarious forms but in itself is a unique reality or force. What, then, is this power, hidden behind the appearances of the world? Schopenhauer believed that his own greatest contribution to philosophical thought lay in giving a definitive answer to this question and thus, as he puts it, clarifying 'the transition from the phenomenon to the thing-in-itself, given up by Kant as impossible'.[56]

55. *Parerga and Paralipomena*, vol. 1, p. 86, footnote.   56. *WWR*, vol. 2, p. 191.

He did this by means of an appeal to inner experience. It is true, he says, that our knowledge cannot penetrate beyond the veil of appearances formed by the qualities and attributes which are all we know of the things of this world, be they animate or inanimate. It is a knowledge of phenomena, of appearances, but not of the essence, the thing-in-itself which lies behind them. 'This essence itself', he writes, 'cannot be understood . . . through any merely *objective* knowledge . . . It would remain eternally a secret unless we had access to it from an entirely different side.'[57] But this entirely different side *does* exist. Kant speaks as though we were knowing beings and nothing more than this—as though we were possessed of absolutely *no* data other than the representations which the mind presents to us as the objects of the empirical world. But this, claims Schopenhauer, is not the case. There is one instance, and one only, in which we have both relative knowledge of the usual kind—that is to say, knowledge of the phenomenon—and at the same time direct intuitive knowledge of the inner nature of the object, immediate experience of the thing-in-itself.[58] This single instance provides the key. It is the essential breakthrough from which we can extrapolate to other objects in the world. And this unique instance, Schopenhauer points out, is ourselves. For each of us, he argues, knows himself or herself in two distinct ways. First, we know ourself as an observable phenomenon forming a part of empirical reality—a human individual with a body existing and operating in the world—just as we know other human beings, animals and inanimate objects. But we *also* have direct, inner, intuitive knowledge of what lies within our body and initiates its actions, and we know from our immediate experience that this factor is our *will*:

In fact, our *willing* is the only opportunity we have of understanding simultaneously from within any event that outwardly manifests itself; consequently, it is the only thing known to us *immediately*, and not given to us merely in the representation, as all else is. Here, therefore, lies the datum alone capable of becoming the key to everything else, or, as I have said, the only narrow gate-

57. *WWR*, vol. 2, p. 364.   58. *WWR*, vol. 2, p. 195.

way to truth. Accordingly, we must learn to understand nature from ourselves, not ourselves from nature.[59]

Like the knowledge of our own existence, Schopenhauer argues, knowledge of the will within us is primary knowledge. It is immediately given to us in self-consciousness. It is the most direct of all our forms of knowledge; a matter of immediate intuition prior to any proof, which each of us knows directly: 'We know and understand what will is better than anything else,' he writes.[60]

What Kant called the *thing-in-itself* and set over against *appearance* (or, in Schopenhauer's language, *representation*), regarding it as something absolutely unknowable, is nothing but what we know immediately and intimately within ourselves as will.[61] The *will* is the single reality which brings into being the entire world—the mysterious 'X' or *thing-in-itself* which lies at the heart of the world of representation, forming the centre of each individual manifestation, giving it its character and binding its attributes together so that we recognize it as a distinct existence. Schopenhauer writes of this insight as 'the most characteristic and important step of my philosophy',[62] and 'the core and main point of my teaching, its metaphysics proper'.[63]

It is hard to do justice to Schopenhauer's conception of the will in a brief study, for while the central idea is strikingly simple, it is the wealth of examples and detail with which he supports it which makes it convincing. What Schopenhauer intends by the word *will* is something vastly greater than we usually understand by the word. We think of willing as being dependent upon knowing, and consequently as something which is limited to conscious beings. Schopenhauer, in one of the boldest moves in the history of philosophy, reverses this order of things, making the will primary and knowledge secondary—essentially a function and instrument of the will. Thus the will, as Schopenhauer conceives it, extends far beyond conscious processes,

59. *WWR*, vol. 2, p. 196.   60. *WWR*, vol. 1, p. 111.
61. *On The Will in Nature*, trans. E. F. J. Payne (Berg, New York, 1992), p. 20.
62. *WWR*, vol. 2, p. 191.   63. *On The Will in Nature*, p. 19.

motivating and controlling the whole of nature. It is the will to live, the will to be, the will to exist as a separate and distinct reality.

This same force which in ourselves we call will, he tells us, is to be found throughout the whole of nature. Starting from those activities which we commonly recognize as being directed by the will, Schopenhauer extends its range first to the unconscious processes (breathing, the functioning of the internal organs, healing processes, etc.) by which animal bodies are sustained; then to the activity of plants, since they too strive to exist and grow; and finally, even to inorganic nature and the universal natural forces such as gravity which control and move it.[64] Thus the will, he says, is 'the key to the knowledge of the innermost being of the whole of nature'.[65] Its expressions range from the unconscious impulse of obscure natural forces up to the most conscious actions of man. In human actions it may often be concealed, but is always present; in animals and their movements we see it in its naked state; in plants we see it as the blind impulse to exist and grow.

Thus every being, every object, is an appearance or phenomenon of the will. But the will itself can *never* be an object, never a representation, for in its essence it does not exist as a phenomenon but at a different level of reality.[66] The will is 'the one and only thing-in-itself, that which alone is truly real, the only original and metaphysical thing in a world in which everything else is only appearance'.[67] Our bodies and the whole process through which they exist are nothing but the phenomenal appearance of the will, its becoming visible, its objectivity.[68] And the same is true of the whole of nature, which in a million different ways expresses the striving of the one, all-pervasive will:

Everything presses and pushes towards *existence*, if possible towards *organic existence*, i.e., *life*, and then to the highest possible degree thereof . . . Let us consider the universal craving for life, and see the infinite eagerness, ease, and exuberance with which the

64. *WWR*, vol. 1, pp. 117–18.   65. *WWR*, vol. 1, p. 109.   66. *WWR*, vol. 1, p. 110.
67. *On The Will in Nature*, p. 20.   68. *WWR*, vol. 1, p. 108.

will-to-live presses impetuously into existence under millions of forms everywhere and at every moment by means of fertilizations and germs . . . seizing every opportunity, greedily grasping for itself every material capable of life.[69]

But the will, as conceived by Schopenhauer, is not confined to the world of organic being: it is 'the innermost essence, the kernel, of every particular thing'.[70] It is the power which lies at the heart of each force of nature and finds expression in every object which arises from these forces: 'In fact', he writes, 'the regular form of the crystal is only the trace of its momentary striving left behind . . . It underlies all the forces of inorganic nature, plays and acts in all their manifold phenomena, endows their laws with force, and, even in the crudest mass, manifests itself as gravity'.[71] So it is, he tells us, that 'we are far more at one with the world than we usually think; its inner nature is our will, and its phenomenal appearance our representation'.[72]

Although the will usually shows itself as an effort to maintain the life of the individual, this is not its real and ultimate purpose. Behind the individual forms which the will takes on lie more fundamental structures, and it is these, Schopenhauer thought, which embody the real meaning of the Ideas which are accorded such a prominent place in the philosophy of Plato; he therefore makes use of Plato's term, *Idea*, while interpreting it in accordance with his own teaching. It is these Ideas, or more general forms of the will, which come into existence as the different species into which living beings are divided. The Ideas are more primary and more powerful than the individual forms which the will takes, and in consequence it is always the maintenance of the species which takes precedence, while the individual is only a means to this end. We see this clearly in the higher species, he says, in the readiness of parents to sacrifice themselves for their offspring; and in the lower forms of life we see it yet more clearly, where thousands of individuals may be sacrificed in order to

69. *WWR*, vol. 2, p. 350.   70. *WWR*, vol. 1, p. 110.   71. *WWR*, vol. 2, p. 293.
72. *WWR*, vol. 2, p. 486.

procure the survival of those few who will ensure the continuance of the species.[73]

That same reason, the paramount importance of the species, explains the strength and vehemence of the sexual impulse. In the act of procreation the will is seen in its purest and most distinct form. When a couple fall in love, Schopenhauer tells us, they may believe they are freely seeking their individual good, but in reality it is the peremptory force of the will which is sweeping through them. It is in order to perpetuate the species and to do so as purely and correctly as possible that we are drawn to certain qualities in the other sex.[74] That is why people in love often have the sensation of being 'swept off their feet' by a force greater than themselves: that is precisely what is happening to them. Among living beings, then, the most concentrated and powerful expression of the will, as it sweeps through matter and imposes form upon it, is to be found in the form of the sexual impulse.[75]

Lastly, this will which is the 'kernel and in-itself of everything', and which everywhere finds expression in the appearances which form the world as representation, is the source of suffering. For to will something is to experience dissatisfaction, to feel a want, a lack, a need. Indeed, suffering is precisely the hindrance or disappointment of the will, just as well-being and happiness are its temporary satisfaction. Moreover, the will is everywhere in conflict with itself, for each separate form that it takes is in its own eyes the only will that matters, and it looks upon everything else merely as objects which may either contribute to or frustrate its own satisfaction. Each separate form that the will takes, each man, animal, plant, or force of nature, tries to assert itself, to seize and dominate matter at the cost of the others.[76] The reality is, Schopenhauer writes, 'a world of constantly needy creatures who continue for a time merely by devouring one another, pass their existence in anxiety and want, and often endure terrible afflictions, until they fall at last into the arms of death'.[77]

73. WWR, vol. 2, p. 354.   74. WWR, vol. 2, p. 539.   75. WWR, vol. 2, pp. 552–5.
76. WWR, vol. 1, p. 309.   77. WWR, vol. 2, 349.

Thus all suffering proceeds from the will—the will to a distinct existence, the will which is in the final analysis the root of the phenomenal world itself. To be subject to the will, to be part of manifested existence, is necessarily and inevitably to suffer. It is, of course, easy enough to dismiss such a view as the outcome of Schopenhauer's particular psychology, and it became common to stereotype him as 'the great pessimist'. Yet it would be an error not to take his view seriously, for this unblinking recognition of the reality of suffering and of its pervasive character is one of the major strengths of his philosophy. Almost alone among Western thinkers of recent centuries he succeeds in confronting the problem of suffering without, on the one hand, seeking to evade or minimize it, nor, on the other, being forced into a materialist or nihilist position.

Schopenhauer himself asserts that the understanding that suffering is an inevitable part of manifestation, far from being unique to himself, is the keynote and original motivation of most of the major religions. He points to early Christianity and early Buddhism as striking examples: in both cases the urge to escape the world, i.e. to sacrifice existence as a separate and individual being maintained by the unceasing affirmation of the will, and to move into that unity known to the mystics and lying beyond self-assertive being, is clearly apparent; strikingly, of course, in the huge monastic movements during the early histories of both religions and in the strong emphasis on the denial of the sexual urge—the very impulse which Schopenhauer had identified as the most distinct manifestation of the will.

Let us now glance back once more at the thought of India: is there to be found in it anything comparable to that mighty and all-pervasive power which Schopenhauer calls the *will*? What comes immediately to mind is the idea, of much importance for both Hindu and Buddhist thought, of *shakti*. This word is usually translated as 'power' or 'formative energy',[78] and the concept it represents plays a central role in the Tantric tradition, although it is by no means confined to it. It is an aspect of Indian thought of which Schopenhauer

78. S. Radhakrishnan: *Indian Philosophy* (Allen and Unwin, London, 1927), p. 735.

can have known little or nothing, for up until the early twentieth century, when Sir John Woodroffe (writing as 'Avalon') drew attention to it in a series of works on the Tantric tradition,[79] there was no reliable account in any European language of what Indians understand by *shakti*. Yet the idea is one of great antiquity and significance in India. Shakti is the power to act which belongs to the Supreme Reality, and without which nothing could take place or exist. She— for the concept is nearly always clothed in mythological forms—is thus one step removed from the Supreme Reality: she is Mahadevi, 'the Great.Goddess', the wife or consort of Shiva, the first stage in the process of manifestation.

Shiva, who is the *Brahman* of Vedanta, the utterly pure Consciousness, is of necessity beyond all activity, for if he acts he is subject to change, hence to relativity and limitation, and would no longer be final Reality. There must therefore be some subordinate power or aspect which brings the world into being. That power, arising somehow out of Shiva but essentially mysterious and beyond the grasp of the mind, is Shakti. A well-known verse of the Tantric tradition tells us that 'Shiva, when he is united with Shakti, is able to create; otherwise he is unable even to move.'[80] Thus Shiva, the absolute Reality, stands ever apart from manifestation which cannot touch him; and it is Shakti which, by apparently and mysteriously limiting that Reality in many millions of ways, produces and maintains all that exists. In its essence, therefore, the role of Shakti is a limiting and negative one; but from the viewpoint of the world this principle of activity appears as supremely positive and creative and is consequently represented as feminine—the source of all living beings, all energies, all forces of nature.

That there is no great distance between this Indian concept of *power* or *formative energy* lying behind the forms of the universe and that of *will* as conceived by Schopenhauer becomes clear from

79. Notable among Woodroffe's works are *Shakti and Shakta*, *The Garland of Letters*, and *The Serpent Power*.

80. *Saundaryalahari*. Cited by S. Radhakrishnan, op. cit., p. 735.

the following definition of Shakti, which is drawn from a modern encyclopedia:

> Shaktas worship Shakti and revere her as the force that makes all life possible and maintains the universe. This is the fundamental creative force whose most primary expression is the sexual energy that unites the polarity of male and female and brings forth new life. Hence the symbols of Shaktism are sexual in nature . . . [Shakti is] the personification of primal energy . . . the dynamic aspect of God through whose agency He creates, maintains and dissolves [the universe].[81]

There is little here that could not apply equally well to Schopenhauer's *will*, while the reference to sexual energy as the primary manifestation of this force is the very point he makes so strongly. Sir John Woodroffe writes that 'Shakti-tattva is also spoken of as the Will (*Iccha*) of Shiva, as yet Unmanifest and inseparable from him',[82] and that '[Shakti] then evolves from Herself the objective world in order that it may be the content of the Shiva consciousness. She is pure Will ever associated with Shiva. She is the seed of the whole Universe of moving and unmoving things then absorbed in Herself.'[83] From such passages it will be apparent how close the Indian concept of *shakti* is to the idea of the will as developed by Schopenhauer: each is the underlying force bringing into being and maintaining the world. Thus we reach the conclusion that the parallel between Schopenhauer's thought and that of India goes considerably further than he

81. *The Encyclopedia of Eastern Philosophy and Religion* (Shambhala Publications, Austin, Mass., 1989), p. 313, s.v. *Sakti.*

82. Sir John Woodroffe, *The Garland of Letters* (Ganesh, Pondicherry, 1985), p. 97.

83. Ibid. p. 109. It is instructive to compare the Tantric description of Shakti with the following passage from the Emperor Julian's *Hymn to the Mother of the Gods*: 'She is the source of the intellectual and creative gods . . . both the mother and the spouse of mighty Zeus; she came into being next to and together with the great creator; she is in control of every form of life, and the cause of all generation . . . she is the motherless maiden, enthroned at the side of Zeus, and in very truth is the Mother of all the Gods' (Loeb Classical Library, *Julian* vol. I, p. 463).

himself or any of his contemporaries were in a position to realize. Not only is his concept of the world as *Representation* paralleled by the Indian idea of *Maya*, but so too is his complementary concept of the *will* by that of *shakti*, the 'formative power' which brings everything into being.

There are further similarities with the thought of India which we can do no more than mention here. The most striking lies in the emphasis which Schopenhauer places upon compassion as the basis of ethics; the close resemblance this bears to Buddhist teaching has often been commented on, and Schopenhauer himself liked to draw attention to it. Closely related to this is his attitude to animals; these, he believed, are often terribly mistreated in the West because of a fundamental misunderstanding of their nature: they too are children of the *will* and in this respect our brethren; it is only the relatively superficial factor of knowledge which separates us from them.

Finally, a word is perhaps in order about Schopenhauer's philosophy as it relates to ultimate reality. In common with Kant, he believed that human thought exists to handle the world of phenomena, and that because ultimate reality is of a quite different order any attempt to grasp it by thought can only fail and mislead. For this reason Schopenhauer carefully abstains from any attempt to describe the nature of ultimate reality and concentrates instead on revealing to us the nature of the world of which we are a part: he seeks to show us what it is, how it works, the degree of reality it has, and the underlying metaphysical force, the will, which brings it into being and keeps it in existence. If he makes no attempt to reach beyond this it is not because he believed there was nothing beyond, but because he was sure that what there is cannot be reduced to conceptual forms: it is, he asserts, the legitimate territory not of reason and the philosopher, but of the mystics.

And so it has appeared to many that for Schopenhauer the *will* is the final reality, the end of the story. This is certainly a misunderstanding, just as it would be a misunderstanding to conclude that for Indian thought *shakti*, the principle of manifestation, is the ultimate reality. For Schopenhauer the real goal to be striven for is not the assertion of the will, but its denial; yet like the Buddha and many other Indian sages he held that since what lies beyond the will—and that means beyond the world—cannot be described it can only be left in silence: 'What philosophy can express only negatively as denial of the will', he wrote near the close of his principal work, '. . . is denoted by the names ecstasy, rapture, illumination, union with God . . . But such a state cannot really be called knowledge, since it no longer has the form of subject and object; moreover, it is accessible only to one's own experience that cannot be further communicated.'[84] For Schopenhauer, as for the Upanishadic sages he studied in the *Oupnek'hat*, final reality is 'that from which words turn back, together with the mind'.[85] There is no doubt that at times his unwillingness to speak of what lies beyond the will has caused confusion in the way his doctrine was interpreted, but we must respect his reasons for doing so.

What we do find is that in the thought of Schopenhauer German philosophy, and with it the thought of the West, approaches closer to India than it does at any other point. Like Schopenhauer, and like the German tradition as a whole, Indian thought seeks its answers not primarily in the external world, but by turning inward to explore consciousness and the nature of mind. Because of this common ground, the thought of Schopenhauer provides us with a bridge which, if carefully used, makes it possible to pass with greater ease and better understanding between the Western philosophical tradition and the world of Indian thought.

84. *WWR*, vol. 1, p. 410.
85. Taittiriya Upanishad 2.4.1.

4

C. G. Jung and the German Tradition

Jack Herbert

THE purpose of this chapter is to show how so many of C.G. Jung's basic ideas in the field of psychology, his fundamental view of the psyche, its structure as well as its functioning—indeed his whole theory of perception—are rooted in ways of thinking and seeing that are specifically German or German-Swiss and which, to a large extent, account for the considerable richness and depth of what he has to tell us. It is a way of understanding Jung which is insufficiently realized; and, although I am not suggesting that this is the only way to approach his life and work (these being amenable to several forms of access), it does seem to me to make good sense to situate them in the culture which gave them birth.

I have called this culture the German tradition because I wish to isolate an inherited mode of thought, a stance towards reality, a *Weltanschauung* if you like, which characterizes this tradition and is at the same time essentially Jungian. This is not to say, of course, that there are not exceptions to, and inevitable variations within, such a well-established procedure, since we are discussing a highly complex culture, such as would be the case with any modern European country. But for the purpose of this essay—and indeed because I believe that the overall argument really holds—I shall try to separate out and describe as clearly as I can the mode of thought and approach to reality marking out this tradition and Jung's appropriation of it.

Briefly it can be categorized as a conviction that it is the mind or psyche which essentially and practically creates our world for us, that it is the mind or psyche through which so-called outside realities are communicated and filtered to us, so that what we actually experience is nothing other, as Jung says, than 'psychic images'. What takes place is no simple, direct transference of outside realities such as that espoused by Locke and British empiricism, whereby a naive realism implies not only the obvious actuality of outside objects, but also the latter's determining role where mind is concerned. The upshot is, as Blake found after studying Locke, that the mind is thereby given a rearranging, associating, basically passive role and status. With Jung, however, as with the bulk of German philosophy (hence the term 'German idealism'), the whole matter is reversed. Mind, psyche, and their constantly creating inner worlds are central and uppermost— which is not to imply that outer reality be ignored. Let us now see what Jung himself has to tell us on this head in a passage from *Modern Man in Search of a Soul*:

> All that I experience is psychic. Even physical pain is a psychic event that belongs to my experience. My sense-impressions—for all that they force upon me a world of impenetrable objects occupying space—are psychic images, and these alone are my immediate experience, for they alone are the immediate objects of my consciousness.... We are in all truth so enclosed by psychic images that we cannot penetrate to the essence of things external to ourselves.[1]

Jung is pointing out here from inside the field of his own discipline that all experience is 'psychic' and that outside objects are inevitably translated into 'psychic images', so that it is the latter we are conscious of, not the objects themselves, as is the case with naive realism. Indeed, elsewhere he can maintain that 'Psyche *is* image',[2] a statement of some significance where the arts of the imagination are concerned. Furthermore, he is very aware of the unnamed natural sciences as being the 'artificial means' whereby we now discover what outside objects are constituted of as separate entities, since we cannot break

1. C. G. Jung, *Modern Man in Search of a Soul* (Kegan Paul, 1934), pp. 219–20.
2. Jung, *Collected Works* 13 (*Alchemical Studies*) (Routledge, 1957–79), p. 50, para. 75.

out of our psyches. In other words, they establish and communicate to us objective features and facts found to be characteristic of external objects, phenomena, matter itself.

In *The Structure and Dynamics of the Psyche* there is another passage which refines and develops these positions in terms of 'the psychological (as against) the realistic standpoint':

> But in order to explain briefly what I mean by the psychological standpoint, I must show that serious doubt can be cast on the exclusive validity of the realistic standpoint. Let us take as an example what a naive mind would consider to be the realest thing of all, namely matter. We can only make the dimmest theoretical guesses about the nature of matter, and these guesses are nothing but images created by our minds. The wave-movements or solar emanations which meet my eye are translated by my perception into light. It is my mind with its store of images, that gives the world colour and sound; and that supremely real and rational certainty which I call 'experience' is, in its most simple form, an exceedingly complicated structure of mental images. Thus there is, in a certain sense, nothing that is directly experienced except the mind itself. Everything is mediated through the mind, translated, filtered, allegorized, twisted, even falsified by it. We are so enveloped in a cloud of changing and endlessly shifting images that we might well exclaim with a well-known sceptic: 'Nothing is absolutely true—and even that is not quite true.' So thick and deceptive is this fog about us that we had to invent the exact sciences in order to catch a glimmer of the so-called 'real' nature of things. To a naive-minded person, of course, this almost too vivid world will not seem in the least foggy. But let him delve into the mind of a primitive and compare his picture of the world with that of civilized man. He will then have an inkling of the profound twilight in which we still live.

What we know of the world, and what we are immediately aware of in ourselves, are conscious contents that flow from remote, obscure sources. I do not contest the relative validity either of the realistic standpoint, the *esse in re*, or of the idealistic standpoint, the *esse in intellectu solo*; I would only like to unite these extreme opposites by an *esse in anima*, which is the psychological standpoint. We live immediately only in the world of images.[3]

This extract, like countless others in Jung's *Collected Works*, restates and reformulates a particular theme or thrust of insight that preoccupies him: it is a means of deepening clarification he is fond of and which I have come to notice. Here he not only repeats his description of our experience as consisting of 'psychic images', but also develops his critique of what he now terms 'the exclusive validity of the realistic standpoint', a fairly all-pervasive view in today's scientific, secular world. From his 'psychological standpoint' he can even go so far as to say with Berkeley that 'there is, in a certain sense, nothing that is directly experienced except the mind itself'. He does, however, qualify matters with 'in a certain sense', and this, as we shall see, is important. But he correctly restates that 'Everything is mediated through the mind, translated, filtered, allegorized, twisted, even falsified by it', so that in order to break through 'this fog about us ... we had to invent the exact sciences in order to catch a glimmer of the so-called "real" nature of things.' We should note, though, that this is only 'a glimmer' and that the word real is placed in inverted commas. For earlier in this same extract Jung has said, in opposition to 'what a naive mind would consider to be the realest thing of all, namely matter', that 'we can make only the dimmest theoretical guesses about' it, something which echoes his previous statement from our first passage above—namely, that 'we cannot penetrate to the essence of things external to ourselves'. This is Kant's position regarding the essential nature of outside objects or 'things-in-themselves' (*Dinge-an-Sich*), as he puts it in his *Prolegomena to any Future Metaphysics*:

3. Jung, *Collected Works* 8 (*The Structure and Dynamics of the Psyche*), pp. 327–8, paras. 623–4.

As the senses . . . never and in no simple instance enable us to know things-in-themselves, but only their appearances, and as these are mere representations . . . all bodies, together with the space in which they are, must be held to be nothing but mere representations in us, and exist nowhere else than merely in our thought. Now is this not manifest idealism?[4]

Kant then maintains that this is not completely the case, since there are good grounds for accepting the reality of 'things-in-themselves', only that we cannot know anything of them as they are. These are what he also called 'noumena', which remain the external source of our experience, and whose reality can only be inferred by experiencing the particular 'phenomena' they release. Essentially, this is Jung's position, for, as he once put it in a letter: 'Epistemologically I take my stand on Kant.'[5] It is likewise, of course, Schopenhauer's, whom Jung had studied intensively.[6]

4. Immanuel Kant, *Prolegomena to any Future Metaphysics*, trans. Peter G. Lucas (Manchester University Press, 1953), section 13, note 11, p. 45.

5. Gerhard Adler and Aniela Jaffé (eds.), *C. G. Jung: Letters 1906–1950*, vol. 1 (Routledge, 1973), p. 294.

6. C. G. Jung, *Memories, Dreams, Reflections* (Fontana Library, 1972), pp. 88 and 117. Referred to hereafter as MDR.

The opening of Schopenhauer's *The World as Will and Representation*, fundamental to our whole argument, should now be quoted, both to point up the connection back to Kant's 'mere representations' (*blosse Vorstellungen*) and the *Weltanschauung* of 'the sages of India':

'The world is my representation': this is a truth valid with reference to every living and knowing being, although man alone can bring it into reflective, abstract consciousness. If he really does so, philosophical discernment has dawned on him. It then becomes clear and certain to him that he does not know a sun and an earth; but only an eye that sees a sun, a hand that feels an earth; that the world around him is there *only as representation*, in other words, only in reference to another thing, namely that which represents, and this is himself. If any truth can be expressed *a priori*, it is this; for it is the statement of that form of all possible and conceivable experience, a form that is more general than all others, than time, space, and causality, for all these presuppose it. . . . Everything that in any way belongs and

To sum up at this point: Jung locates reality not in the material objects of the outside world but, as we saw in the passage cited above from *The Structure and Dynamics of the Psyche*, in the 'conscious contents that flow from remote, obscure sources'. He rounds off the cited passage with the following summarizing statement:

> I do not contest the relative validity either of the realistic standpoint, the *esse in re*, or of the idealistic standpoint, the *esse in intellectu solo*; I would only like to unite these extreme opposites by an *esse in anima*, which is the psychological standpoint.

Fundamentally, he is arguing for 'the middle way' between the two extremes of *esse in re* and *esse in intellectu solo*, a position which he names *esse in anima* and which, he asserts, unites the first two, designating it 'the psychological standpoint'. However, this is also a very German standpoint in terms of its thinking via opposites that have then to be united and thus in some way transcended.

Goethe stands on the same ground, as already noted in Chapter 2, with his theory of life conceived as a constant process of polar opposites and their fusion at a higher level—what he calls 'polarity and intensification' (*Polarität und Steigerung*); something that Coleridge had likewise grasped through his early reading of Jakob Boehme and his later study of German idealist philosophy while at Göttingen.[7]

------

can belong to the world is inevitably associated with this being-conditioned by the subject, and it exists only for the subject. The world is representation.

This truth is by no means new. It was to be found already in the sceptical reflections from which Descartes started. But Berkeley was the first to enunciate it positively, and he has thus rendered an immortal service to philosophy . . . . On the other hand, *how early this basic truth was recognized by the sages of India*, since it appears as the fundamental tenet of the Vedânta philosophy ascribed to Vyasa, is proved by Sir William Jones in the last of his essays.

(*The World as Will and Representation*, trans. E. F. J. Payne, Dover Publications, New York, 1969, vol. 1, pp. 3–4. Emphasis added).

See also n. 22 below, and the exposition in Chapter 3 above of Schopenhauer's concept of the world as representation.

7. See the quotation from M. H. Abrams cited at the end of Chapter 2 above and the passage from Coleridge cited there by Abrams; see also Chapter 2, n. 86.

The emphasis in both cases is on a dialectically upward progression and is encapsulated in Goethe's own term, *Steigerung*, related as it is to the verb *steigen*, meaning 'to climb or ascend', yet signifying a qualitatively 'heightening' or 'enhancing' process, such as we find in alchemy. Indeed, the term as Goethe intends it undoubtedly possesses alchemical overtones, since the goal of alchemy is itself achieved through a complex, oppositional procedure of 'dissolve and coagulate' (*solve et coagula*) applied a number of times to the 'primary substance' (*prima materia*), while simultaneously refining it, so that we get an upward progression.[8] Thus a German love of dialectical thinking via opposites would seem to be alchemical in nature;[9] and essentially this is what we find embodied in Jung's theory and principle of individuation, 'the process by which a person becomes a psychological "individual", that is, a separate, indivisible unity or "whole"'.[10] For, as he explains in his autobiography, *Memories, Dreams, Reflections*:

As I worked with my fantasies, I became aware that the unconscious undergoes or produces change. Only after I had familiarized myself with alchemy did I realize that the unconscious is a process, and that the psyche is transformed or developed by the relationship of the ego to the contents of the unconscious. In individual cases that transformation can be read from dreams and fantasies. In collective life it has left its deposit principally in the various religious systems and their changing symbols. Through the study of these collective transformation processes and through understanding of alchemical symbolism I arrived at the central concept of my psychology: the process of individuation.[11]

8. See the passage from M. H. Abrams's *Natural Supernaturalism* referred to in the previous note.

9. One need only think of 'the central idea of the Hermetic procedure: the "conjunction of the opposites" (*coniunctio oppositorum*)'—Johannes Fabricius, *Alchemy (The Medieval Alchemists and their Royal Art)* (The Aquarian Press, 1989), p. 55—and compare it with Nikolaus Cusanus's theory of the *coincidentia oppositorum* and Hegelian dialectics.

10. *MDR*, p. 414.   11. *MDR*, p. 235.

Alchemy and psychology are thereby seen to join hands, with a significant awareness of and emphasis on that central activity of change, process and transformation characteristic of both disciplines.

However, note that before he was able to get this far, Jung's main conception of the nature and function of the human psyche was such, I believe, as to lead him in this direction:

> Just as all energy proceeds from opposition, so the psyche too possesses its inner polarity, this being the indisputable prerequisite for its aliveness, as Heraclitus realized long ago. Both theoretically and practically, polarity is inherent in all living things.[12]

The position presented here is basically that of the *yin/yang* symbolization of life's forces in Taoism, a fact which doubtless accounts for the intuitively enthusiastic reception in 1928 of 'the manuscript of a Taoist-alchemical treatise entitled *The Secret of the Golden Flower'* sent to the psychologist by Richard Wilhelm,[13] and of which he then said: 'Light on the nature of alchemy began to come to me only after I had read the text of the *Golden Flower',*[14] words which recall the 'Oriental Renaissance' discussed in Chapter 1.

Now it is easy to see that however much Jung maintains, as he does quite vociferously, that his approach to dealing with the psyche and its problems is that of 'an empiricist first and foremost',[15] his view of their nature and functioning is anything but empiricist. To begin with, it is sufficient to notice his surprise on experiencing the following after reading a book on *Fichte's Psychology and its Relation to the Present*, for which he wrote a foreword:

> Naturally I am familiar with Leibniz, C. G. Carus, and von Hartmann, but I never knew till now that my psychology is 'Romantic' . . . I hold that, in spite of all abstractions, objectivity, absence of bias, and empiricism, everyone thinks as he thinks and

---

12. *MDR*, p. 379.   13. *MDR*, p. 222.   14. *MDR*, p. 230.

15. Jung, *Collected Works* 18 (*The Symbolic Life*), p. 770, para. 1731, from the *Foreword* to *Fichte's Psychology and its Relation to the Present*.

sees as he sees. Accordingly, if there is a type of mind, or a disposition, that thinks and interprets 'romantically', analogous conclusions will emerge no matter whether they are coloured by the subject or by the object.[16]

One recalls a comparable statement of Blake's, where he is defending in a letter his own kind of painting and vision: 'I see Every thing I paint in This World, but Every body does not see alike. . . . As a man is, so he sees. As the Eye is formed, such are its Powers'.[17] Nevertheless, as Jung was a practising doctor and psychiatrist concerned with healing, we get an approach to mental illness and psychological problems, a methodology in short, which is scientific and empirical: hence, 'grounded in experience'. Again:

I approach psychological matters from a scientific and not from a philosophical standpoint. Inasmuch as religion has a very important psychological aspect, I deal with it from a purely empirical point of view, that is, I restrict myself to the observation of phenomena and I eschew any metaphysical or philosophical considerations.[18]

Statements of a similar nature can be found scattered throughout the *Collected Works* in order to stress the fact, thereby defending himself from his critics, that, whatever his findings about the nature of the psyche turn out to be, they are neither those of a metaphysician nor a mystic, but those of a doctor, psychiatrist, and longstanding explorer of the inner worlds, who has simply been reporting over the years what he has discovered. However (and this is the decisive point), Jung's emergent concept and view of the psyche, in line with the names referred to above—namely, Leibniz,[19] Carus, and Hartmann—are not those endemic to the empiricist account. So let us

16. Jung, *Foreword* to *Fichte's Psychology*, p. 771, para. 1732.
17. William Blake, Letter to the Revd Dr Trusler, 23 August 1799.
18. Jung: *Collected Works* 11 (*Psychology and Religion: West and East*), pp. 1–2, para. 2.
19. On once being asked about empiricism's view of the mind, taken over from scholasticism's 'nothing in the intellect which was not first in the senses' (*nihil in*

now listen to Jung himself as he describes and unpacks the key empiricist concept of the mind—that of Locke's *tabula rasa*, the mind as 'blank or razed tablet' given us at birth or, quoting Locke himself, 'white paper, void of all characters'; hence, in Jungian terms, without 'innate ideas' and not even 'pre-formed' (*vorgeformt*):

> The psyche of the child in its preconscious state is anything but a *tabula rasa*: it is already pre-formed in a recognizably individual way, and is moreover equipped with all specifically human instincts, as well as with the *a priori* foundations of the higher functions.[20]

And more substantially from *Psychological Types* (1921):

> One likes to think of the human mind as, originally, a *tabula rasa* that gradually gets covered with perceptions and experiences of life and the world. From this standpoint, which is the standpoint of empirical science in general, an idea cannot be anything else but an epiphenomenal, *a posteriori* abstraction from experiences, and consequently even feebler and more colourless than they are. We know, however, that the mind cannot be a *tabula rasa*, for epistemological criticism shows us that certain categories of thinking are given *a priori*; they are antecedent to all experience and appear with the first act of thought, of which they are its pre-formed determinants. What Kant demonstrated in respect of logical thinking is true of the whole range of the psyche. The psyche is no more a *tabula rasa* to begin with than is the mind proper (the thinking area). . . . Hence the new-born brain is an immensely old instrument fitted out for quite specific purposes, which does not only apperceive passively but actively arranges the experiences of its own accord and enforces certain conclusions and judgements. These patterns

---

intellectu quod nisi prius in sensu), Leibniz is reported as having replied: 'Yes—nothing apart from the intellect, that is!'

20. MDR, p. 381.

of experience are by no means accidental or arbitrary; they follow strictly pre-formed conditions which are not transmitted by experience as contents of apprehension but are the preconditions of all apprehension. They are ideas *ante rem*, determinants of form, a kind of pre-existent ground-plan that gives the stuff of experience a specific configuration, so that we may think of them, as Plato did, as *images*, as schemata, or as inherited functional possibilities which, nevertheless, exclude other possibilities or at any rate limit them to a very great extent.[21]

Here it is clear that, regarding the nature of mind or psyche, Jung is quite consciously 'anti-scientific' in terms of science's traditional, run-of-the-mill account of consciousness. For, as he states, from 'the standpoint of empirical science in general, an idea cannot be anything else but an epiphenomenal, *a posteriori* abstraction from experiences'. That is, it is 'epiphenomenal' in the sense of being derived simply from phenomena and the world of experience: hence secondary, incidental, and subordinate to experiences from outside—*a posteriori* or 'from what comes after' implying the dependency or contingency of ideas as effects created by outside causes. The crucial event which demolishes this reasoning is, for Jung, the 'epistemological criticism' he refers to, which is, of course, Kantian: 'What Kant demonstrated in respect of logical thinking is true of the whole range of the psyche.' This assertion tells us that Jung has accepted Kant's revolutionary account of mind[22]—his so-called 'Copernican revolution'—and extended it to cover the whole of the psyche.

This involves realizing, not that 'our knowledge must conform to objects', as with Locke, but on the contrary that 'objects must conform to knowledge', since it must be clear on reflection that the sensibility and understanding underlying and guiding our perceptions are already sufficiently structured and unified to make sense of the

21. Jung, *Collected Works 6 (Psychological Types)*, pp. 304–5, para. 512.
22. Revolutionary, that is, for this whole period of Western philosophy; not for India, of course, as Schopenhauer has pointed out. See n. 6 above.

external world. Apperception or inner awareness, just like its polar opposite, perception or outer awareness, is certainly both structured and unified, as Kant and Jung both knew; whereas for empiricism there is only loose association. Yet as Jung contends in the passage above, the human brain 'does not only apperceive passively but actively arranges the experiences of its own accord', with 'these patterns of experience (being) by no means accidental or arbitrary'. Here he is very close to the *Gestalt* psychologists working in Frankfurt around 1910—Wolfgang Köhler, Max Wertheimer, and Kurt Koffka— whose researches into the science of perception resulted in their discovery that we perceive in terms of configurations, patterns, or holistic units of sensed experience—what they termed 'forms/shapes' (i.e. *Gestalten*). We can best illustrate this by comparing the structure and composition of a soap-bubble with those of a pile of coins. Whereas a soap-bubble is an organized whole from which nothing can be subtracted or added to, since it bursts, a pile of coins can be subtracted from and added to at will without disturbing the pile. The latter is an aggregate of things, atomistic if you like, not a fused synthetic whole. An aggregate of things would then be an empiricist model of the mind and psyche—a fused synthetic whole a Jungian model, with the *Gestalt* theory of perception applied to the overall psyche.[23] So a pile of coins versus a soap-bubble.[24] And in this connection it is worth mentioning that Coleridge saw the nature of fancy, as opposed to that of the imagination, as consisting in 'the aggregative and associative power'.[25] Like Jung, of course, he had

23. *Gestalt*, as well as the more usual *Form*, is a word Jung also applies to 'archetype', his own term for those primal creative denizens and constellations in the psyche: e.g. 'the archetype, which in itself is an irrepresentable, unconscious, pre-existent form that seems to be part of the inherited structure of the psyche' (*Collected Works* 10 (*Civilisation in Transition*), p. 449, para. 847); and 'The archetype in itself is empty and purely formal, nothing but a *facultas praeformandi*, a possibility of representation which is given *a priori*. The representations themselves are not inherited, only the forms . . .' (*Collected Works* 9(i) (*The Archetype and the Collective Unconscious*), p. 79, para. 155).

24. Cf. here the neurologist R. L. Gregory in his *Eye and Brain: the Psychology of Seeing* (1977): 'Each of us literally does create his or her own world.'

25. Samuel Taylor Coleridge: *Biographia Literaria*, ed. Nigel Leask (Everyman, 1997), p. 168.

studied his Kant. In passing, I would merely like to add that I have more and more come to believe that the simplistic empiricist model of mind has had very negative consequences in the field of artistic and intellectual form, making us unlikely to rise much beyond the level of sense-impressions, things, and facts, together with their accumulation and amalgamation. On this head, the English Jungian, H. G. Baynes, in his *Analytical Psychology and the English Mind*, registers this comparative insight:

> It is not without interest that, for the practical Anglo-Saxon mind, the word *reality* is derived from *res, thing*; whereas with the more introverted German mind the word *Wirklichkeit* derives from *wirken, to effect*. What has effect upon the mind, whether coming from within or without, is therefore the basis of reality for German psychology: not just the thing as such.[26]

Baynes, incidentally, knew Jung well, having been his assistant for several years and accompanying him on his expedition to Africa.

To sum up at this point: Jung's view of the psyche is that it is not at all a random, haphazard affair based on the vagaries of intake from outside, but on the contrary reveals 'a kind of pre-existent ground-plan that gives the stuff of experience a specific configuration'.[27] In this sense it can be said to possess an aesthetic structure in the manner of a work of art; and in similar fashion, as we shall see, it is concerned with meaning and purpose—hence qualities not quantities. Finally, to clinch what we said earlier about the 'psychic image', Jung in his *Psychological Types* has this to tell us:

> When I speak of 'image' in this book, I do not mean the psychic reflection of an external object, but a concept derived from poetic usage, namely, a figure of fancy or fantasy-image, which is related only indirectly to the perception of an external object.[28]

26. H. G. Baynes, *Analytical Psychology and the English Mind* (Methuen, 1950), p. 226.
27. Cf. 'a kind of pre-existent ground-plan' with 'an irrepresentable, unconscious, pre-existent form' in n. 23 above.
28. Jung, *Collected Works 6 (Psychological Types)*, p. 442, para. 743.

So far we have emphasized the primacy of mind and psyche in Jung, together with the tradition they stem from, their structured nature and function, and their relation to outside reality in terms of perception theory. We now have to bring in the unconscious and its role, something which sits, of course, at the very heart of Jungian psychology and of which he remains a great advocate like Freud before him. In his autobiography he states that 'Our basis is ego-consciousness, our world the field of light centred upon the focal point of the ego', but that 'closer study shows that . . . the images of the unconscious . . . have a reality and spontaneity of their own', although 'we regard them as mere marginal phenomena'.[29] Jung then goes on to say that, by virtue of two key-dreams he has just had—those emissaries of the unconscious—he has been forced to reverse this position:

The aim of both these dreams [was] to effect a reversal of the relationship between ego-consciousness and the unconscious and to represent the unconscious as the generator of the empirical personality. This reversal suggests that in the opinion of the 'other side', our unconscious existence is the real one and our conscious world a kind of illusion, an apparent reality constructed for a specific purpose, like a dream which seems a reality as long as we are in it. It is clear that this state of affairs resembles very closely the Oriental conception of Maya.[30]

The primacy of the unconscious announced here is not only the result of Jung's own self-analysis[31] and its substantiation in the extensive work carried out at the Burghölzli Mental Hospital in Zurich, but has also been prepared for by a whole way of thinking that has roots going back to the Romantics, Boehme, and the German mystics. Even with such an Enlightenment figure as Leibniz, we find an accreditation of subliminal awareness to the mind in the form of so-called

29. MDR, p. 356.   30. Ibid.
31. See MDR, Ch. 6: Confrontation with the Unconscious.

petites perceptions. We then, crucially, get Fichte, 'for (whom) the light of consciousness emerges out of the dark of the unconscious', as Lancelot Law Whyte says in *The Unconscious Before Freud.*[32] And Fichte himself has written: 'The apperceptive faculty of the mind is an activity which contains the ultimate basis of all consciousness, but never itself comes to consciousness.' Again, there is Schelling's *Natur-philosophie* with its principle of the 'eternally unconscious' (*ewig Unbewusste*); and, already mentioned, C. G. Carus, physician and painter friend of Caspar David Friedrich, with his seminal work *Psyche* (1846), the opening sentence of which runs: 'The key to the understanding of the character of the conscious lies in the region of the unconscious.' Further, at many points in *The World as Will and Representation* Schopenhauer anticipates both the Freudian and Jungian unconscious with his key concept of the will. And Goethe's earlier recognition of the role of the unconscious and the power of the daemonic are, of course, central here. Finally, much later, we get Nietzsche's famous outburst against the 'absurd overestimation of consciousness [in the West] as the supreme kind of being, as God'; and more specifically:

> Consciousness only touches the surface . . . . The great base activity is unconscious. Every sequence in consciousness is completely atomistic. The real continuous process takes place below our consciousness; the series and sequences of feelings, thoughts, and so on, are symptoms of this underlying process.[33]

With all this at the back of him, let alone Freud's discoveries as expounded in *The Interpretation of Dreams* (1900), it is little wonder that the structure and workings of the unconscious should dominate in Jung's writings.

At this juncture, and staying for the moment with the topic of dream-interpretation, let me introduce some comments made by

---

32. L. L. Whyte, *The Unconscious Before Freud* (Tavistock Publications, 1962), p. 120.
33. For both Nietzsche quotes see L. L. Whyte, pp. 175–6.

Kathleen Raine in a brilliantly compact foreword to a Routledge edition of Jung's work on *Dreams* (2002); this book is a conspectus drawn together from his vast and varied writings on dream analysis and dream symbolism. Dr Raine makes several key-points which reinforce my line of argument, while also bringing in others I have not touched on. She begins by saying that 'In the course of the twentieth century . . . I would say without hesitation that the greatest change in the mental experience of the modern West has been the discovery (or rediscovery) of the inner world of the psyche.' Jung's major role in effecting this change is obviously in the forefront of her mind, but behind it is the German tradition as a whole as well as the influence of India, as we saw in the previous chapter. Kathleen Raine goes on to point out that 'To Jung we owe the discovery that the psyche is structured, controlled by archetypes corresponding to what in earlier civilizations were known as the "gods".'[34] These archetypes, the structuring potencies and forms of the psyche, were found to live deep in the centre of our inner worlds, and as psychic principles and powers to rule and/or conflict within just like the gods and goddesses of myth. Hence Jung's great love and knowledge of mythologies, fairytales, legends, and epics, with their original cultural base founded on the education he received first at Basel Gymnasium, then at the university there, where Nietzsche, Jakob Burckhardt, and J. J. Bachofen, author of the once-influential *Mother Right* (*Das Mutterrecht*, 1861), had lectured. From Bachofen Jung would have learned much about tomb-symbolism as well as other things; and it is important to note that his concept of the archetype initially derived from Burckhardt's use of the term 'primordial image' (*urtümliches Bild* or *Urbild*), as he himself made clear: 'What I understand by it is identical with the "primordial image", a term borrowed from Jakob Burckhardt . . .',[35] while at the same time he traces its history from St Augustine to Schopenhauer. Jung then draws out the analogy with the latter much further:

34. Jung, *Dreams* (Routledge Classics, 2002), p. xix.
35. Jung, *Collected Works* (*Psychological Types*), p. 377, para 624.

For Schopenhauer the idea is a visual thing, for he conceives it entirely in the way I conceive the primordial image. . . . (He) clearly discerned that the 'idea', or the primordial image as I define it, cannot be produced in the same way that a concept or an 'idea' in the ordinary sense can . . . . There clings to it an element beyond rational formulation, rather like (his) 'temper akin to genius', which simply means a state of feeling. One can get to the primordial image from the idea only because the path that led to the idea passes over the summit into the counter-function, feeling.[36]

What is especially fascinating about this passage is that we learn that Jung's archetypes, like Schopenhauer's Ideas, are both feeling-tinged and visually conceived, unlike the rational concepts of Kant; with the result that they comprise, for Jung, two opposed psychic functions—thinking and its 'counter-function, feeling', thereby issuing in a fusion of two polar opposites: a *complexio oppositorum*, to use one of his favourite Latin formulations. It is significant here that, as a Jungian colleague has pointed out, there are very few references to music in the *Collected Works*,[37] whereas the visual is everywhere present. For instance, we get splendid, symbolically rich illustrations to several of the main volumes, plus the visual descriptions and recountings of myths and fairytales, and the interpretations of a multitude of symbols—in particular, the alchemical ones.[38] Finally, with regard to a major Jungian symbol of wholeness, the *temenos*, whether viewed as an actual sacred precinct enclosing temple, church, or mosque, or as an inner *temenos* found in dream-analysis, we find that a visual architecture, or at the very least an enclosed space, is always evoked.[39] In fact, it is this complex visual legacy deriving not

36. Ibid., p. 438, para. 734, and pp. 446–7, para. 753.
37. Provided by Roland Hindmarsh, co-founder of The Cambridge Jungian Circle (1992).
38. Consult in the *Collected Works*—vol. 5, *Symbols of Transformation*; vol. 9(i), *The Archetype and the Collective Unconscious*; vol. 12, *Psychology and Alchemy*; and vol. 13, *Alchemical Studies*.
39. Consult vol. 12 of *Collected Works*.

only from Jung's cultural background, but also from his own and his patients' dream-worlds, which enriches and deepens so much of his psychology.

Another important point which Kathleen Raine allows to emerge from her foreword is the contrast Jung makes between 'the causal approach of Freud' vis-à-vis dream-interpretation and his own so-called 'final' approach. In this connection she quotes a central passage from Jung:

> From the standpoint of finality the images in a dream each have an intrinsic value of their own . . . It recognizes no fixed meaning of symbols. From this standpoint all the dream-images are important in themselves, each one having a special significance of its own, to which, indeed, it owes its inclusion in the dream . . . .: it does not conceal, it teaches.[40]

Relating dream-images and situations back to their ostensible causes entails the procedures of empirical science, and Jung takes due stock of this; but he then goes on to remark:

> The causal point of view is obviously more sympathetic to the scientific spirit of our time with its strictly causalistic reasoning. Much may be said for Freud's view as a scientific explanation of dream psychology. But I must dispute its completeness, for the psyche cannot be conceived merely in causal terms but requires also a final view. Only a combination of points of view—which has not yet been achieved in a scientifically satisfactory manner, owing to the enormous difficulties, both practical and theoretical, that still remain to be overcome—can give us a more complete conception of the nature of dreams.[41]

Jung's stance, here as elsewhere, is fair-minded yet critically appraising. And he himself, wherever he thinks it valid and necessary,

40. Jung, *Dreams*, pp. 33–4.   41. Ibid., p. 35.

makes use of empirical methods, as in the case of what he terms 'the relatively fixed symbols' which, he says, 'are individually marked by subtle shifts of meaning'; and 'it is only through comparative studies in mythology, folklore, religion, and philology that we can evaluate their nature scientifically'.[42] One notes the range of disciplines called for and the emphasis placed on the fact that meaning and evaluation are accentuated.

This brings me to my next point—namely, that Jung's psychology is essentially concerned with interpreting and evaluating what he designates as 'psychic phenomena' and not, like Freud, with what causes these. Jung is never causally reductive and, as he maintains in *Psychology and Religion: West and East*: 'My standpoint is exclusively phenomenological, that is, it is concerned with occurrences, events, experiences—in a word with facts.'[43] But these are 'facts of mind', as Coleridge understood them, and which for both men possessed just as much validity as the natural facts of the outside world, as well as being for Jung himself of equal status to biological specimens and laboratory findings, even though he was fully aware of the subjective factors involved. Again, as he often used to stress: 'Psychology cannot establish any metaphysical "truths", nor does it try to. It is concerned solely with the phenomenology of the psyche.'[44] Yet since the establishing of the individual psyche's phenomena is empirically carried out and documented, whereas, by contrast, interpreting and evaluating all this entails, from Jung's point of view, meaning, purpose, and qualitative difference, therefore something radically other is called for—which is where the German tradition of hermeneutics comes in. Starting with the late eighteenth-century exegesis of scriptural texts by J. G. Eichhorn, biblical scholar and orientalist, who provided the Victorians with the term 'the higher criticism', and with Friedrich Schleiermacher, the Protestant theologian who was the first to develop a theory of 'general hermeneutics' as 'the art of understanding', a long

42. Ibid., p. 107.
43. Jung, *Collected Works* 11, p. 2, para. 4.
44. Jung, *Collected Works* 18 (*The Symbolic Life*), p. 309, para. 742.

and distinguished tradition of interpreting written texts reaching far beyond the scriptures was inaugurated, which has continued right up to the present day with figures such as Hans-Georg Gadamer, protégé and friend of Heidegger, himself a key-thinker in this tradition. It is difficult to gauge to what extent Jung was influenced by all this. On the other hand, it is equally difficult to see how he could have avoided it, especially when we take into account a passage like the following from a 1953 letter to Henry Corbin:

> Your intuition is astounding: Schleiermacher really is one of my spiritual ancestors. He even baptized my grandfather—born a Catholic—who by then was a doctor. . . . The vast, esoteric, and individual spirit of Schleiermacher was a part of the intellectual atmosphere of my father's family. I never studied him, but unconsciously he was for me a *spiritus rector*.[45]

In this connection it is worth reflecting that, like Schleiermacher, Jung was born into a Lutheran pastor's family, a cultural social unit which throughout the nineteenth and twentieth centuries was responsible for producing a galaxy of talents—and not only theologians—such as Lessing, the Schlegels, Nietzsche, and others; so that there is a sense in which Jung's lifelong attempt to 'penetrate into the secret of the personality', as his autobiography puts it (hence learning how to read its meanings and interpret its images and symbols), represents an extension of hermeneutics into the field of the psyche.

In J. J. Clarke's highly informed *In Search of Jung* (*Historical and Philosophical Enquiries*) we are alerted to the fact that the brilliant hermeneutical philosopher, Wilhelm Dilthey (1833–1911), was lecturing at the University of Basel during the 1860s and that, although Jung nowhere mentions him, it is most unlikely he knew nothing about him. The decisive point to stress regarding Dilthey's probable significance

---

45. Gerhard Adler and Aniela Jaffé, (eds.), *C. G. Jung: Letters 1951–61*, vol. 2 (Routledge, 1976), p. 115. In this letter Jung also states: 'I don't belong to the auditory type', thereby confirming Roland Hindmarsh's finding above.

for the psychologist is that, starting out from Schleiermacher, he shifted the whole domain of hermeneutics from interpreting scriptural texts to encompassing the humanities or *Geisteswissenschaften*. These could and did include all cultural artefacts and modes of creative expression from symbols, paintings, buildings and works of literature, to cultural–psychological patterns and configurations as these manifested themselves artistically and socially, as well as religious beliefs. Dilthey's total area of scholarly interpretation was astonishing and is mirrored in his textual approach known as 'the hermeneutic circle': this involved the principle that, in order to understand and hence interpret any text (and, by extension, any aesthetic product), you have to understand and can only understand the entire work via its individual units of meaning and, vice versa, each unit of meaning only in the light of the entire work and what it implies. Hence there is an inbuilt circular process, as M. H. Abrams has remarked:

> Dilthey maintained . . . that the hermeneutic circle is not a vicious circle, in that we can achieve a valid interpretation by a sustained, mutually qualifying interplay between our progressive sense of the whole and our retrospective understanding of its component parts.[46]

His approach was therefore both detailed and holistic, and one can certainly find similarities here to Jungian readings of the psyche, its constellations and images. However, Dilthey was supremely aware of the role played by the historical and cultural contexts out of which texts and works of art arise, as well as the relevance of adjacent fields of study in helping to determine or corroborate levels of meaning. J. J. Clarke even goes so far as to suggest that the Dilthey method of using interpretatively 'a continual oscillation between text and context, comparing one with the other' is highly reminiscent of Jung's 'principle of

---

46. M. H. Abrams, *A Glossary of Literary Terms* (Holt, Reinhart & Winton, 1981), p. 84.

amplification'—that is, one of the psychologist's procedures for interpreting dreams, defined in the glossary to his autobiography as:

Elaboration and clarification of a dream-image by means of directed association . . . (i.e. spontaneous ideas which proceed from a given dream situation and constantly relate to it) . . . and of parallels from the humane sciences (symbology, mythology, folklore, history of religion, ethnology, etc).[47]

More fundamental still are Dilthey's discovery and promotion of the principle of 'understanding' (*verstehen*) in grasping the nature of the *Geisteswissenschaften* as opposed to the principle of 'explaining' (*erklären*) appropriate to the natural sciences, the *Naturwissenschaften*. Unlike explaining, understanding is seen as involving the activation and implementation of other faculties than those required for scientific explanation; and especially perhaps in German, keeping in mind the cognate form, *Verständnis*, signifying a sympathetic understanding for particular situations, persons, or things.[48] Further—the process of *verstehen* for Dilthey entails an imaginative 'experiencing and/or afterwards experiencing' (*erleben* and/or *nacherleben*) of the particular art-work, text, cultural event or movement. So, in all this, he can be seen as providing the humanities and works of art not only with a very different rationale from that used in the sciences, thereby assigning them to a contrary sphere of being, but also, through his emphasis on *erleben/nacherleben*, opening the way to psychological, inner-spiritual dimensions. It is this mode of thought, this kind of cultural approach, which is perhaps best able to indicate where Jung is coming from.

Then, bearing in mind his family and educational–cultural background, it is also possible to see how Jung's preoccupation with the unconscious, and his discovery of a 'collective' apart from a 'per-

47. MDR, pp. 410 and 412 (from the *Glossary* provided by Aniela Jaffé).
48. *Verständnis* can include emotional as well as intellectual understanding, as in the English—'He is a very understanding type of person.'

sonal' terrain existing and functioning there, can become both 'the matrix of a mythopoeic imagination which has vanished from our rational age'[49] and the location of 'the existence of a God-image'.[50] One notes, of course, the linkage being made here between 'a mythopoeic imagination' and the presence 'of a God-image'.[51] Of the latter, the glossary to *Memories, Dreams, Reflections* states that it is 'a term derived from the Church Fathers, according to whom the *imago Dei* is imprinted on the human soul'. Thus, in specifically Jungian terms: 'When such an image is spontaneously produced in dreams, fantasies, visions, etc., it is, from the psychological point of view, a symbol of the self, of psychic wholeness.'[52] In *Psychology and Religion: West and East*, Jung adds: 'The God-image does not coincide with the unconscious as such, but with a special content of it, namely the archetype of the self. It is this archetype from which we can no longer distinguish the God-image empirically.' And finally from the same volume: 'One can, then, explain the God-image . . . as a reflection of the self, or, conversely, explain the self as an *imago Dei* in man.'[53]

Now a preoccupation with and continual searching to locate the God within is something endemic to both German mysticism and German music: one thinks of Meister Eckhart, Hildegard von Bingen, Nikolaus Cusanus, Boehme, Angelus Silesius, F. C. Oetinger and others, whose overall impact is taken up into Romanticism; while in the second field we get Bach, Schütz, Beethoven, Brahms, the Wagner of *Parsifal*, and other composers through to Stockhausen.[54] For my present argument, however, what is noticeable in all this is the shift away from religious dogma and theology *per se* to the sacred within

49. *MDR*, p. 213.   50. Jung, *Dreams*, p. 66.

51. Both the mythic and the sacred possess of necessity qualities of transcendence, pointing towards the beyond; and essentially the imagination is also engaged in such an activity—transforming mundane reality and unifying things. Hence, as Jung says of the God-image: it is 'an archetype of wholeness'.

52. *MDR*, p. 413.   53. Jung, *Collected Works* 11, pp. 468 and 190.

54. Cf. Thomas Mann here in his essay, *Deutschland und die Deutschen*: 'For abstract and mystical—that is to say, musical—is the German relationship to life' (*Denn abstrakt und mystisch, das heisst musikalisch, ist das Verhältnis des Deutschen zur Welt*) (*Gesammelte Werke* 11 (S. Fischer Verlag, 1960), p. 1132).

the realm of human experience. This certainly had roots in the Lutheran–Pietist tradition and Romanticism's re-discovery of a sacred dimension both in wild nature and in the inner world of man. At the same time, it did not prevent most of the significant theology from the modern period being conceived alongside it. Generally speaking, and not only in Germany, there was at this time a concentration of the religious in personal experience, away from institutions and external authorities, as witness William James's *The Varieties of Religious Experience* (1902)—highly influential in its day and symptomatic of the shift of focus to religion's experiential side, soon to be further opened up in such key-works as Rudolf Otto's *The Idea of the Holy* (1917) and Martin Buber's *I and Thou* (1923). This can now be seen as an area in which Jungian psychology would have found itself at home, exhibiting several similarities that suggest a kind of symbiotic relationship, as disclosed by this extract from *Memories, Dreams, Reflections*:

Our psyche is set up in accord with the structure of the universe, and what happens in the macrocosm likewise happens in the infinitesimal and most subjective reaches of the psyche. For that reason the God-image is always a projection of the inner experience of a powerful *vis-à-vis*. This is symbolized by objects from which the inner experience has taken its initial impulse, and which from then on preserve numinous significance, or else it is characterized by its numinosity and the overwhelming force of that numinosity. In this way the imagination liberates itself from the concretism of the object and attempts to sketch the image of the invisible as something which stands behind the phenomenon. I am thinking here of the simplest basic form of the mandala, the circle, and the simplest (mental) division of the circle, the quadrant or, as the case may be, the cross.[55]

Apart from the overall thrust of this paragraph, with its emphasis

55. *MDR*, p. 368.

on 'the God-image' and 'the inner experience', the use of 'numinous' and 'numinosity' comes straight from Rudolf Otto, whose coinages they were. Furthermore, Otto defines the numinous as what he terms a 'contrastive harmony' (*Kontrast-Harmonie*),[56] a description strangely reminiscent of Pico della Mirandola's Renaissance definition of beauty's mysterious quality as 'a "composite" and inherently "contrarious" principle: *una concorde discordia*'.[57] Pico further defines it as a '*mysterium tremendum et fascinans*', a fusion of opposites anticipating what Jung later called 'the *complexio oppositorum* of the God-image', out of which 'a synthesis of the opposites within the psyche' can result in that age-old symbol of the mandala signifying 'the *wholeness of self*' or, 'to put it in mythic terms, the divinity incarnate in man'.[58] Rudolf Otto, a distinguished Sanskrit scholar who had travelled to India, was already talking of the mandala as 'a magic circle of images used for purposes of contemplation' (*ein magischer Bilderkreis für Kontemplationszwecke*); so that, all in all, it does seem as if both Otto and Jung were mining the same veins of ore. Martin Buber, too, with his dialogical account of religious experience and relationship via his 'I–Thou' (*Ich–Du*) and 'I–It' (*Ich–Es*) interchanges, is not far removed from the same area of concern: one thinks of the holistic and interactive nature of the 'I–Thou' realm as opposed to the objective functionalism of the 'I–It' relationship characteristic of the modern world—let alone the importance of the former for psychotherapy.

Early on in this chapter I mentioned the connections between alchemy and Jung's psychology, and we all know of his deep and intensive study of the alchemical tradition over many years. I quoted his statement that 'through understanding of alchemical symbolism I arrived at the central concept of my psychology: the process of individuation'; and though, of course, alchemy is by no means a German creation, from Paracelsus onwards the German contribution

---

56. See Rudolf Otto, *The Idea of the Holy*, trans. John W. Harvey (Oxford, 1928), pp. 42–3, where the aesthetic category of 'the sublime' is put forward as an analogy.

57. Consult Edgar Wind, *Pagan Mysteries of the Renaissance* (Penguin, 1967), p. 78.

58. MDR, p. 367.

to it has been paramount and its impact and sustained influence on the country's culture and thinking considerable. Let me therefore conclude by quoting once again from Kathleen Raine's foreword to Jung's *Dreams*:

> Alchemy is the mythology which Jung made most use of in his thought and practice, and this places him within the tradition of German imaginative thought and practice, Goethe in particular, and the remarkable history of German philosophy and Romanticism.[59]

59. Jung, *Dreams*, p. xxii.